THE LIFE STORY OF
LESTER SUMRALL

The Man

The Ministry

The Vision

THE LIFE STORY OF
LESTER SUMRALL

Lester Sumrall

as told to
Tim Dudley

New Leaf Press

Library of Congress Catalog No. 92-64449
ISBN: 0-89221-229-2

Edited and written by Rob Kerby and Val Cindric

Dedication

To Cliff Dudley, founder and CEO of New Leaf Press.

God spoke to him, and after personally visiting with me, he was accumulating the material for this book at the time of his death. This book was his personal project.

Tim Dudley, president of New Leaf Press, accepted the challenge of his father's labor, and saw this book through its completion after his father's passing.

To the entire Dudley family, thank you for your labor of love, and God bless you.

Lester Sumrall

CONTENTS

Publisher's Preface

While working on the book with Brother Sumrall, I heard him say he had never been out of the will of God in sixty-three years. He wasn't boasting; he was stating a fact. His ministry testifies to his obedience to the Spirit of God and the call on his life.

In Romans, it says that because of the disobedience of one, we are all sinners, but because of the obedience of One, we are all made righteous.

One man obeying God can still result in thousands coming to Christ. Obedience is a powerful force, and Lester Sumrall's life exemplifies its effectiveness. Over the years, thousands, possibly a million souls have been touched one way or another by the obedience of this one man.

We consider it an honor and privilege to publish his life story. My prayer is that while you read this book, you will become even more willing to follow the call on your own life — guided by the example of Lester Sumrall's life.

Tim Dudley,
Publisher

1

The Battle for My Young Heart

My mother had decided, even before I was born, that I was going to be a preacher. She had prayed for me fervently while I was in her womb — back when I couldn't do anything about it, except kick a little!

Saved as a teenager and later baptized with the Holy Ghost at a tent revival, my mother had her heart set on being a missionary. Circumstances changed the direction of her life when her sister died, leaving behind a husband and three young children. Realizing her niece and nephews had no one to take care of them, my mother selflessly agreed to move in with the family.

However, her widowed brother-in-law immediately set his sights on marrying her — his deceased wife's sister. In an effort to woo her he pretended to become a Christian. My mother, believing that he loved her and Jesus Christ, married him and gave up her dream of going to the mission field.

Conflict soon developed. My mother spent much of her time in Bible study and attending, what they called in those days, the Ladies' Prayer Group. My father, however, scorned Mother's quiet devotion to the Lord.

Oh, he'd go to church. Seventy-five years ago, everybody went to church. But during Sunday dinner, he'd criticize the pastor and complain about his preaching. In spite of all the hell-fire and brimstone sermons he heard week after week, my father continued to smoke, drink, chew, and live a sinner's life.

I was born at home, child number six and completely unplanned. My father, who had decided they should stop at five, always considered me an accident. Once he told me bluntly, "You weren't supposed to be here."

My half-brothers Houston and Kerney, my half-sister Anna, my brother Ernest, and my sister Louise were all much older than I. Sister Leona, who was number seven, was born a few years later after we had moved back to Laurel, Mississippi. It was there my father found work in the railroad roundhouse.

All day he made things out of glowing steel, hammering molten metal on his iron anvil beside a raging blacksmith's forge. For a man who worked with his hands, he always made good wages and, as far back as I can remember, we always had an automobile. In fact, for many years we were the only family on the block that owned one.

With enormous muscles and a commanding voice, my father was a giant in my eyes. In fist fights, all he needed was one punch and the other man was finished. I once watched him lift a grown man, and the chair he was sitting in, into the air with one arm.

When he took me to the barber shop for my first haircut, the barber placed me on a small stool on the chair and wrapped a cloth around my neck. He asked, "Well, sonny, how do you want your hair cut?"

I looked up at him and said, in a proud, self-assured voice, "Just like Daddy's." The men in the barber shop burst out laughing.

I was embarrassed, but what else could I say? I

wanted to be just like my daddy.

When Daddy spanked me, he paddled the daylights out of me, but I only remember that happening two or three times. Mostly he just yelled at me; he wasn't abusive, but he did seem cold, demanding, and even mean at times.

On the playground, I was a pint-sized version of him. I fought every kid in the neighborhood, even taking on boys four inches taller than myself with little injury. Punching fast and furiously, I would beat the daylights out of them until they were bloody all over.

I also fought God, probably because I knew I had a choice to make.

My mother was a gentle, kind, and godly woman. I loved her and wanted to please her, but I didn't want to be like her because that meant I had to be good.

On the other hand, if I followed in my father's footsteps, I could be my own boss and do whatever I pleased.

While the inner battle raged, I dug in my heels, determined to be like my daddy.

I worshipped him from afar, accepting his indifference toward me and modeling myself in his image. My feelings toward him were mixed, even confused at times. I don't recall him ever bouncing me in the air or holding me close. I don't remember him hugging me or saying, "I love you, Lester."

But my mother did, every day. She was the one who dried my tears and doctored my scrapes. When I rushed home with excited tales that every little boy likes to tell, she was the one who listened. It must have grieved her sometimes to see the trouble I got into.

When I wasn't fighting, I was playing marbles, and nobody could beat me. From ten feet away, I could aim at a marble and hit it every time. This skill soon became very profitable since I would win everybody's marbles and then sell them back.

One morning I left home with a box of marbles and

wandered around the neighborhood. A kid stopped me and said, "I'll trade you my knife for some marbles." So I traded him.

Another looked at the knife and said, "I'd sure like to have that knife." So I traded it for something else.

Before three o'clock I was back home with a billy goat and a beautiful billy goat wagon.

My father exclaimed, "Where did you get that?"

I said, "Well, I've forgotten the address right now, but I traded it."

For the first time in my life, I saw Daddy nod his head in approval. For a brief moment, I felt he was proud of me.

Making money came naturally. On my way home from school, I would buy a hundred-pound sack of peanuts, roast twenty or thirty pounds, shaking them every minute or two so they were cooked all the way around. Then I'd fill little bags with roasted peanuts and go to the nearby sawmill where I'd sell them for five cents a bag. I'd often come home with a dollar or two, which was more than some men were making in a day.

Before long, I had more money than anybody at our house. My brothers and sisters always came to me if they needed a loan. I became my family's junior banker and I charged interest, too.

When summer came, instead of selling peanuts, I devised another money-making scheme. After constructing a small wagon, I purchased a hundred pounds of ice and some heavy syrup — grape, strawberry, vanilla, and other flavors. Then I paid a little boy fifty cents a day to pull my wagon while I walked behind ringing a bell and calling out, "Snowballs!" At the end of the day, I would come home with three or four dollars.

Even as a youngster, I soon figured out that if you wanted to spend money, you had to make it first. My father had never given me a dollar in his life, so I knew if I was going to have any money, I had to make it myself. Besides, I sensed Daddy's silent approval of my business ventures. I didn't expect him to praise me outright. That just wasn't his way.

In fact, we seldom knew what Daddy was thinking — except when revival time came at the church.

Mother's pastor would come to her and say, "Sister Sumrall, we have nowhere to put the preacher. Won't you let the evangelist stay with you? He'll just use one room, him and his wife and kids. The kids will sleep on the floor."

I guess everybody figured that since my father made a good living and had a car, our house was the best place for them. Of course, my mother had a hand in it, too. She loved having preachers — and their entire families — board with us.

Sometimes those evangelists and their wives and three or four kids stayed at our house for three months. They had meetings every night, and people would come from everywhere to hear them. Hundreds would find Christ as their Saviour, and a whole community would change. It was revival time!

That's when Daddy would go into high gear. "Those preachers are nothing but con-artists and charlatans!" he'd rant, and I'd nod in agreement when my mother wasn't looking. My daddy thought that if you didn't sweat or pound steel or plow in the fields, then you weren't really working.

In those days evangelists were usually dirt poor and couldn't even afford to stay in hotels. That's why they lived in the homes of the church people. I don't know why I didn't realize that those poor preachers certainly weren't getting rich. But if Daddy said it was so, then I believed it.

My father would come home to find strangers sitting around in the living room, and he'd bellow, "Who is this?"

"It's the evangelist. He's going to bless our home," Mother would reply.

Then my father would start cursing and say, "Why they're nothing but beggars, too lazy to work, traveling around like kings! All they do is meddle in people's lives and get rich passing the hat."

Well, I liked that kind of talk! That sounded good, so I went around spouting out the same verbiage. Like my father, I had nothing but scorn for all those preachers my mother brought into our house. Sometimes I had good reason to complain.

Our table wasn't big enough to seat everyone at the same time, so Mother would serve the evangelist and his family first. If I got anything at all, it was the scraps when that bunch got through eating. No sir, I didn't like that at all.

They always took over my bedroom, so I had to sleep on the floor on blankets. If the preacher hung his trousers on my bedpost, I'd steal money out of the pockets and go off and spend it.

One day a friend and I let the pastor's son tag along when we went swimming. Winter rains had swollen the creek and the high water was dangerous, but, still, we dove into the muddy current, daring each other to follow.

I swam about halfway across when, suddenly, the flood waters started to pull me under. I fought, but the water was cold and the current too strong.

As I struggled to keep my head above water, I remember that the preacher's son panicked and was screaming, "Let's get home! We're in trouble! He's gone!" Then he ran off, leaving my friend to feel around in the cold, muddy water until he found me.

Desperately, my buddy dragged my body out onto the bank. I wasn't breathing since my lungs were filled with water. Somehow he punched my back until the mud and water gushed out. I wheezed back into the world of the living.

The preacher's kid got a whipping for running out on us, and I swore I would never befriend another one of those sissies. From that time on, I gave every preacher's kid who had the misfortune to stay with us every reason to resent their fathers' ministry.

Of course, the poor kids had rough lives with no home — living three months here, three months there, one month over there. Nevertheless, I had no sympathy for any of them.

The preachers and their families didn't have an easy time at our house. But instead of returning my hatred or taking revenge, they would simply look toward heaven and pray, "God, help Lester. God, save Lester."

I just sneered under my breath, "Yeah, well, you get out of my house, and God can do a lot better with me."

2

The First Time I Heard God's Voice

Just before I turned ten, my brother Archie was born. For the first time, I saw a different side of Daddy. Overnight, it seemed, my hard-hearted father became a gentle giant, tender and affectionate toward his newborn son. I was amazed to see him rocking the baby in his arms and carrying him around the house.

Daddy taught Archie how to walk and even let the toddler sit in his high chair right beside him at the dinner table. *It's all right*, I told myself, *after all, there's a big age difference between me and the baby. Besides, Archie adores him.*

Then before his second birthday, Archie died.

My father didn't cry; he just stared in stony silence. Even at the funeral everybody else wept, but not Daddy. When he got home that day, he suddenly burst into tears and laid on the floor, sobbing as if his heart would break.

Then he got up and said God had spoken, telling him, "You can go where Archie is, but you can't bring him back. You have to make the decision."

At church, my father shared with the congregation what God had told him, and Mother began to believe that Daddy might get saved. But he didn't change because he wouldn't submit his heart to the Lord.

My mother was an unrelenting prayer warrior. From my earliest years, I remember hearing her take all her needs and burdens to God and "travailing" — earnestly seeking the Lord for hours and days — particularly when faced with family difficulties for which there were no earthly solutions.

After Archie died, she would say, "Lord, you took my little one, but you gave me my husband." I didn't understand how she could thank God for my daddy when he made life so difficult for her. More than once, however, I heard her ask God to help her be grateful for his good points. She fasted and prayed for her husband to get saved, but she never preached at him.

It was with the death of Archie that the Lord began to soften my father's heart. For the first time there seemed to be a crack of light coming from his hardened soul.

In spite of her submissive nature, Mother was a fighter — a spiritual warrior. One night while kneeling in prayer by a chair in the front room, she looked around to see an angry lion. Something told her that the lion was the spirit of her husband and that she had to defeat it first before her prayers could be answered. As she prayed, the demonic spirit started to move backward. "Get out of this house!" she kept commanding until it backed out through the door.

Although the answer to her prayers for my father's salvation was long in coming, my mother's spiritual labors over her children bore fruit early. As the spiritual leader of our family, she had consistently instilled in all us children the importance of a personal faith in Jesus Christ and our responsibility to serve Him.

The two oldest boys, Houston and Ernest, started preaching when they were fifteen or sixteen. By the time I was eleven, Ernest was attending Central Bible College in Springfield, Missouri.

The school was so pleased with his accomplishments

that, upon his graduation, they gave him a tent, a piano, and benches so he could be an evangelist. Traveling all the way down to Mississippi, he did conduct a few revivals. But Ernest was more of a teacher than an evangelist, and he later became a successful church pastor and settled near Mobile, Alabama.

About that time, my father had a terrible accident. While he was working with a piece of hot metal, it flew up in the air and hit him in the eye, completely destroying his eyeball. After a short stay in the hospital, he was sent home where, for many, many weeks, he just writhed in pain.

Because Daddy couldn't work, money soon ran out and so did the food. Even when we had nothing, my mother would say to all of us kids, "Let's get busy and set our table."

"But, Mother, we don't have anything in the house to eat," we'd complain.

"Don't say that," she would answer. "Say, 'God is going to provide.'" Then Mother would set the table and put a glass of water at every plate. "Now we are going to sit down and pray, and God will send us the food." She seemed to have an extra measure of faith.

Sure enough, anywhere between ten minutes to twelve and twelve o'clock, somebody would come to our door carrying a basket full of hot food. Mother would graciously accept the meal and put it on the table.

Every time she took that step of faith, without fail, someone in the community would be moved to help us and think, "We'd better bless the Sumralls. That man's sick." They didn't know we were out of money and food, but Mother never doubted that God would speak to their hearts and meet our needs.

My mother was a great intercessor who spent hours in, what was literally, her "prayer closet." In those days, people would take their winter clothes and blankets and put them in a special closet until it got cold again. Even if

Mother was in the house by herself and didn't need privacy, she'd go in there and kneel down and pray.

Many times I would come home from school and call for her.

"What were you doing?" I'd ask, noticing the tears in her eyes and knowing where she'd been.

"I was praying."

"What are you praying for?"

"Oh, I'm happy," she'd reply with a smile and that's all she'd say.

I really didn't give her answer much thought since I considered praying and religion to be for women and weaklings. At the time, I didn't recognize what a fighter my mother was.

The Ladies' Prayer Group met in our home every day. This odd-looking lot of women wore long-sleeved dresses with old-fashioned collars that came up to their chins and hems that covered their shoes. But when those women began to pray, they shook heaven and hell. They knew how to do spiritual battle as I discovered at an early age.

As a child I had suffered from pellagra, a sometimes fatal disease caused by a deficiency of niacin and protein in the diet. Today it occurs mostly in Third World countries. At times my skin became so inflamed all I could do was scream with pain. It got so bad that the pellagra affected my digestive system, making it impossible for me to eat. The doctor said I would die.

That's when the Ladies' Prayer Group began to storm heaven on my behalf. After daily doses of their hands-on praying and intercession, God healed me, and I quickly recovered.

My faith in God, however, remained superficial in spite of the fact that Mother took me to every church meeting — Wednesday night, Sunday morning, Sunday night — and even some afternoons.

The pastor's sermon every Sunday night was, "Jesus

is coming soon." Man, he could preach, but it was always, "Jesus is coming soon."

Then the preacher got sick and died.

"Jesus didn't come soon enough," I scoffed to myself. But I knew better than to let my mother hear me say such a thing.

The next preacher who came had virtually the same message, "These are the last days! Jesus is coming soon." He died, too.

A third one came along and began to preach, "Jesus is coming soon."

I thought, *These preachers are a bunch of liars — with all this "coming soon" stuff.*

One Sunday night as I sat there in my pew, the Lord said to me, "Would you like to know when I'm coming back?"

"Well," I answered — too young to think it strange that God was talking to me, "I've been thinking on it a long time."

He said, "I'm going to tell you. It's in Matthew 24:37. 'But as it was in the days of Noah, so shall it be in the day of the coming of the son of man.' Noah was 500 years old when I said, 'Build the ark.' He was 600 years old when he went into the ark."

God continued, "My mercy is one hundred years."

I began to cry.

He said, "I gave them one hundred years to repent, and they didn't want to repent. So they had to be judged."

I said, "And it's going to be that way in the end of time?"

The Lord said, "Yes."

"When did You start counting?" I asked impudently.

I waited for an answer but all I got was silence. Why? Because God never responds to stupidity. That's the reason He doesn't talk to most of us.

It was a long time before I heard from God again, but that didn't mean He wasn't trying to get my attention.

One day as I was walking on the railroad tracks, a boxcar started rolling downhill toward me, but I didn't hear it. My older brother saw it and ran like the wind. With no time to even yell a warning, he hit me like a football player, knocking me off the track. We both fell into the ditch as the boxcar rattled past.

He saved my life, but, still, I didn't think much about it. Why should I? I considered myself to be indestructible.

Not long after that incident, our family moved to Panama City, Florida, where all the kids, including me, practically lived on the beach. Coming mostly from fishing families, they played in the ocean all the time. Some days we stayed in our swimsuits from morning until night.

One day, I decided to make a raft, so I told all the kids to collect every big, fifty-gallon drum they could find. Then we roped them together and laid boards across them, working for hours. Finally, I had everybody push the raft out into the deep water, where I announced, "Well, there's our new diving platform."

At that point, one of the boys looked at me and growled, "Who made you the boss of this thing?"

"I'm not the boss," I answered.

"Well, then how come ever since we started, you've made every one of us obey you?"

"Well, you shouldn't have obeyed," I said simply.

"Yeah, but we had to."

I didn't realize that I had directed the entire project from beginning to end. "Oh, is that right?" I asked smugly, feeling somewhat pleased by the idea that when I told people to do something, they did it.

That day, something happened inside me, and I felt good about myself and my natural ability to lead others. My mother had recognized these leadership qualities, too, but the way she wanted me to use them was quite different from what I had in mind.

On her knees, Mother saw in me the missionary that

she had so longed to become. At first she had thought my half-sister, Anna, would fulfill the calling to the mission field when she expressed an urgency to take the gospel to China. But Mother's dreams were once again dashed when Anna disobeyed the Lord and married a non-Christian.

When my sister Anna died at an early age, the heartache of what could have been weighed heavily on my mother. She was determined that I would obey the Lord's call, just like my older brothers had.

But being a missionary or preacher was the farthest thing from my mind. I still wanted to be like my father in spite of the fact that he didn't seem to care what I did. Too bad I couldn't see that my mother's godly life was much more deserving of imitation than my father's rebellious ways.

Mother was no weak-sister Christian. She was a much tougher disciplinarian than my father. She never said, "Just wait 'til your daddy gets home." When we needed a switching, she gave it to us and didn't bother him with our wrongdoing and punishments.

Mother ran the house and made most of the household decisions. When Daddy got his paycheck, she put it in the bank and paid all the bills.

As the center of our family, Mother also provided the spiritual leadership for us children. In fact, she taught us the Bible every night. When we could quote all the books of the Bible by memory or recite the Twenty-Third Psalm without hesitating or name the twelve Apostles or the judges of Israel, she'd give us a prize. Somehow all that Bible teaching never got down into my heart, probably because I never let it.

Whether I wanted to or not, Mother continued to drag me off to her spirited revival services where I sat with my head down, refusing to sing or listen. Angry that I wasn't playing with my friends, I would doze off on the hard pews while the preacher droned on and on long into the night.

Even when confronted with incredible miracles of healing, I was not impressed. But there was one incident that I never forgot.

My mother had an open, bleeding cancer in her breast. In those days the doctors had only one form of treatment for cancer — cut it out. They told my mother, "Even if we operate, we can never get the roots, and it'll come back. Let us know your decision."

Not knowing what to do, my mother did what she did best — she prayed.

One night after she had gone to bed, she saw Jesus walk into the bedroom. He didn't say anything, just touched her and smiled.

The next morning, she told the family, "I'm healed of that cancer. Jesus was in my room last night."

My father just grunted.

Three or four mornings later, however, he asked, "You haven't mentioned that cancer in several days. When are you going back to the doctor?"

"Well, tomorrow is the regular time to go back to have it dressed," my mother answered. "I think I'll check it myself. The doctor won't mind I'm sure."

When she went to her room and pulled back all the bandages, there in the gauze lay something that looked like a little baby octopus. It had a core or center to it, and out from it went things like little strings — the tendrils of the cancer. Then she looked in the mirror and saw that a new piece of skin, like a baby's skin, had grown across the hole.

When she showed my father the cancer laying on the piece of gauze, he could not deny what had happened. She excitedly told us children, and the church, too — and anybody who would listen. She lived another 45 years, using every opportunity to witness about God's miracle-working power and grace.

Even my old, racist grandfather, a Confederate veteran of the Civil War, didn't escape my mother's prayers.

A widower who could no longer live alone because of a stroke, he came to stay with us for a while. Since he couldn't even feed or clothe himself, my mother was taking care of him. And she took care of him the best way she knew how! She called on the Ladies' Prayer Group.

Now my grandfather wasn't what I would call a Christian. In fact, I considered him to be just plain mean.

Seeing him sitting slumped over in the wheelchair brought back one of my earlier memories. He had dressed up in his faded Confederate uniform and stood on the front porch, spewing forth for us grandchildren to hear, his hatred for every Yankee and every black man living. Now, even in his old age, he nurtured an aching vengeance that could not be satisfied.

But that didn't deter the Ladies' Prayer Group. One day all eight or ten of them stood around his wheelchair and asked, "Mr. Chandler, do you believe in God?"

"Yes."

"Do you believe in Jesus?"

"Yes."

"Do you believe in healing?"

"Yes."

"Now give your heart to Jesus."

They led him in a sinner's prayer and then began to pray for him. Right there, in the front room of our house, the power of God came on my grandfather. The Spirit of the Lord touched him and went throughout his whole body.

Suddenly, the old man came up out of that wheelchair, when before he couldn't walk a step, and began to walk. His arms, which had been limp, began to move. And that was it! He was healed!

He soon returned to his own home, where for the next fifteen years my grandfather did his own cooking and took care of his house. A housekeeper did come in maybe once a week to clean, but, otherwise, he took care of himself.

One night I was at his house, and my grandfather went off to bed at his regular time of eight o'clock. My brother and I were sitting in another room when we heard a little struggle. We went in to check on Grandfather, but it was too late. He was already gone. Without sickness and without any great problem, he just left this world.

That night I couldn't help but remember the day the Ladies' Prayer Group had visited my grandfather. I saw my bitter old Rebel granddaddy who couldn't walk or feed himself fully healed and made well. That had an impression on me as a boy and built faith into my heart. It had an effect on me, but it wasn't enough.

I continued being a delinquent.

As I grew older, I cussed and smoked and dropped out of school at age sixteen. My friends were no good. Many times my mother threatened that if I didn't stop stealing and getting into trouble, she was going to put me into a reform school.

Several of my friends were either shot to death robbing stores, murdered running moonshine, or on the losing side of shoot-outs with the police. Some of them killed each other.

But me, I thought I was indestructible.

I wasn't gonna be no sissy like those women in the Ladies' Prayer Group.

I was a man like my daddy.

3

Out of the Belly of the Whale

S hortly after I dropped out of school, I began spitting up blood at night. I didn't tell anybody at first, but one morning my mother saw my pillow and asked, "What's that blood doing on there?"

"Oh, I coughed." But I knew something was terribly wrong.

When the blood was there every morning, she took me to our doctor, who lived a few houses from us. He gave me a checkup and said what I already knew — I had tuberculosis.

Tuberculosis was a death sentence in those days.

"Well," he told my mother and me, "since we are neighbors, I can see you every day, so there's no use in taking him off to a hospital. Anything I can do for him there, I can do here."

So, he came to see me every day.

I'm sure he wondered, as I did, how I contracted the disease. We lived right on the beach and my room had many windows, so I had plenty of fresh air and sunshine. I should have been a healthy sixteen year old.

I began getting weaker and weaker. The flesh just

rolled off of me until I weighed about ninety-three pounds. I was just a stack of bones. Soon I could not get out of bed.

My mother's Ladies' Prayer Group started coming in to pray and lay hands on me. They were persistent, standing around the bed, pleading with the Lord to spare my life.

I told my mother to call off her prayer partners. "Don't bring that bunch of old women back in here anymore." But the next week, they'd be back.

My mother, so persistent, would usher the women into my room where they would stand around the bed and say some of the silliest things like, "Oh, God, why does this dear little innocent child suffer?"

I would stick my head under the covers and cuss them. If I would have cussed them outside of the covers, my mother would have given me a strapping in bed.

Underneath the covers, I said, "I'm nothing that you think I am. I'm not innocent, and I'm not little. I don't want you in here. Just get out."

On my seventeenth birthday I had been lying in bed for several months. I was bleeding from the lungs, coughing up my life. I had a fever that they couldn't break.

I was dying.

About four o'clock I began to cough and heave up big chunks of my lungs. It was getting bad. I turned purple, and my mother told my sister, "Run get the doctor. Lester's getting worse."

He came running over and tried to take a pulse and to get a little pinch of blood. Then he took my mother aside and said, "I can't get anything out of this boy. Nothing. He doesn't have any pulse, and I can't get any blood out."

Grimly he looked at my mother and said, "Call your husband. This boy is dying."

The whole family came into my room. Over to one side, the doctor told them in a whisper, "In two hours this boy will be dead. That's the death rattle in his throat right now, and that bluishness in his face means he's not getting enough blood to his brain for his body to live. He's going to die tonight."

He put his hand on my father's shoulder and said, "Now, Mr. Sumrall, I'm going back to the office, and I'll write out his death certificate and sign it. You can pick it up tomorrow morning and get a place in the graveyard for him. They won't sell plots out there unless you have a certificate, so I'll leave it on my desk."

My mother began crying.

I couldn't hear what they were saying, but I knew what was going on. My father looked grim and my mother was weeping, so I figured out that doctor had said something very bad.

I thought, *When the doctor leaves, the jig's up. I'm going to die.*

As he walked out the door, I began to panic.

I was seventeen years old! My life had run out before it had started. I wasn't ready.

But I was dying — and I was scared.

I hung onto life.

Sometime during that dark night, I looked up, and on one side of my bed I saw a coffin just my size, open and tilted. The insides were covered with soft, white satin, and it was empty, waiting for me. I knew it was mine.

I looked at it, and I thought, *Oh, there's my coffin. It's very pretty all right, except I don't want that.*

I turned my head the other way, and there I saw the biggest Bible in the world. It stretched from the floor to the ceiling beside my bed, and the letters on the page stood up high.

I looked, and God said, "That's My Word. You will have to select one of these tonight."

I said, "Oh, yes, Lord. I'll go to church and I'll get right."

God said, "No, you've told me that before. Tonight, you will take THAT coffin, or THAT Book. I want you to preach My Word, or you're going to die tonight."

Well, like most Southerners, it was my nature to stall when being pushed to make up my mind. I preferred to leave a hard decision for tomorrow if I could, rather than face it today.

I replied, "Lord, I'm going to do that someday."

The Lord said, "You are! Right now! There are no more sunrises for you. No more daylight for you. You are either going to be put in that casket, or you are going to take My Word and proclaim it."

"Well, Lord, I don't want to die," I answered. "I'm afraid to die. I'm not ready to die. So, evidently I'm going to take the Word, the Bible."

I did not hear an audible voice, yet it was as distinct and firm as any I had ever heard. God was giving me a choice.

I despised preachers and the thought of being one made me cringe, but I was terrified at the thought of dying. That floating coffin meant much more than just a grave. It meant everlasting, eternal hell. I had heard enough preaching to know that.

Looking straight at the Bible, I prayed, "God, if the only way in the world for me to live is to preach — then, I'll preach."

Then, to confirm what I had just said, I added. "If you will let me live as long as I preach, one day I will be the oldest man in the world because I won't ever stop preaching."

Then a miracle took place. Inside of me something happened.

I knew that if I said "yes," it would forever be "yes." That was the first time in my life I had ever had a feeling like that.

Normally if I said "yes," ten minutes later it could be "no," and it was none of your business. I did as I pleased, and that's why I got into so much trouble. You never knew what I would do next because I changed my mind to suit myself.

But that night something happened.

Something happened in my belly, and I said, "God, I'm sorry for my sins, and I'm sorry that I mistreated everybody. I'd like for You to forgive me." At that moment, I felt something take place down inside of me.

Now, I didn't submit my heart to the Lord that night. I didn't pray the sinner's prayer. I just agreed to preach.

My heart was still filled with rebellion. I hadn't asked the Lord to save my soul or baptize me with the Holy Spirit.

I just made a deal with Him. I agreed to preach. It was a business agreement with the Lord. If it meant I would live, then I would preach. I had made a firm commitment to God, a covenant — and I meant it.

I drifted into a sweet, deep slumber, and while I was asleep, the Lord healed me.

The next morning when I opened my eyes and looked around, I saw my mother standing over my bed. Her eyes were blurry from crying, and I could tell she hadn't slept much that night.

"I'm hungry," I said.

"Oh," she said, "I'll get you some grape juice."

"I've had all the grape juice I can swallow for a long time."

"What do you want?"

"I want exactly what Daddy had for breakfast."

Down South, years ago, when we had breakfast — we had breakfast! We didn't just smile at the table; we had huge homemade biscuits covered with white gravy along with eggs and ham and grits.

I said, "That's what I want."

"No, you haven't had any solid food for weeks. You would die if you ate that," my mother argued.

I looked up at her with a funny little smile and said, "That may be, but I'm gonna die full of ham, eggs, hot biscuits, gravy, and grits! Go get it!"

"Well, I've always heard that you are supposed to

give a person their last request," my sweet mother said. "The doctor said you're gonna die, and no doubt you are delirious."

She didn't know I was healed. There was no blood on the pillow that morning, but she didn't look to see.

From that day on, not another drop of blood came out of my mouth. I never did have that fever again. It was gone. I was healed by God.

With the idea that a dying person should have what they want, Mother went and cooked it all up, put it by the side of my bed on a little table, and left the room. She didn't want to watch my futile attempt to eat solid food.

Getting up on my elbow, I reached over and began to eat. I ate everything on that plate. It was as if you'd called in the cat, and he had licked it. There wasn't a thing left but a clean plate.

My mother came back and said, "Where's all that food?"

I pointed at my stomach and said, "In here."

"All of it?" she asked, amazed.

"That's not all. I want some more."

"Well," she said, "not now. You just let me talk to the doctor about this and see what he says."

"I'm all right," I answered. "You don't need that doctor no more. Last night I saw a vision. I saw a coffin. I saw a Bible. I'm going to be a preacher."

Now, I was the meanest kid she had or even knew. She had spanked me more than the rest of the family put together. She had threatened to send me away to a reformatory, but here I was talking about preaching.

She went delirious with joy.

She wept, and she cried and said, "Oh, God. Can it be? Can it be?"

"Yeah, I'm healed. I'm strong. I'm not weak anymore."

She rejoiced and began proclaiming the good news of my healing to the whole family. Nobody else believed it, but three days later I was walking all over the house. Strength just flowed back into me.

Ten days later a neighbor boy of ours came by and said, "Say, you want to go fishing?"

"Sounds good to me," I replied, and we went out on the Gulf of Mexico and fished all day. We came back with enough mullet to make quite a bit of money.

Some days we'd fish; other times we caught crab or dug for oysters.

Three weeks later God spoke to my heart and said, "Did you promise Me that you would preach?"

"I did," I answered.

"Well, get to doing it then!" He commanded. "Don't delay it. Do it now."

I rushed downstairs where my father was having his breakfast. "Daddy," I declared to him, "I'm gonna preach. And I'm going today."

He stared at me in disbelief.

Then he stood up. "You're not going to do any such thing," he roared. "You're not strong enough to go. You wouldn't know anything to say if you did go."

I told him I was plenty strong and had lots to say.

"I'm not going to have you begging for a living," he thundered. "I want you to have a real job."

"Daddy, I've got to go preach."

"You're not going to do it!"

"God said I had to."

"God nothing!" he declared.

Skinny seventeen-year-old that I was, I stood there trembling. Then I turned and ran back upstairs to my room.

"You'll starve to death if you do!" my father bellowed after me. Then as he gathered up his things to go to work, he hollered up the stairs, "Boy, I'll take care of you when I get back home."

In my room, I fell to the floor, weeping. "My heavenly Father says 'Go,' and my earthly father says 'No!' "

I prayed. "What can I do?"

Through my tears, God impressed upon my mind Isaiah 41:10-11. I didn't know what it said, but He told me to find it.

I opened my Bible and read: "Fear thou not; for I am with thee."

Instantaneously, God took the fear out of me.

Until that moment, my stomach had been shaking; I had been so afraid. When I read "Fear thou not," the fear drained out of me. God said, "I am with thee."

I knew Daddy wasn't going to like it if I disobeyed him, but God said, "I am with thee: be not dismayed."

I had been told that I couldn't preach and that nobody wanted to hear me say anything. I was plenty dismayed.

Looking back at Isaiah 41, I continued reading: "For I am thy God: I will strengthen thee; yeah, I will help thee; yeah, I will uphold thee with the right hand of my righteousness. Behold, all they that were incensed against thee shall be ashamed and confounded; they shall be as nothing; and they that strive with thee shall perish."

When the Lord gave me that Scripture, I got up off the floor, filled with great peace. God's love absolutely overwhelmed me. He reached down and took fear out of my being. Suddenly, I was laughing and crying at the same time. It took me about an hour to regain my composure.

"Okay, Lord," I said aloud. "If You're with me, I'm ready to go."

I got dressed and looked around the room for my belongings. In the closet I found a little brown suitcase, the kind made out of thin fiberboard with two little buckles that snapped the sides closed. It didn't take long to fill it with all my earthly possessions and what few clothes I owned.

My father had already left for work when I marched downstairs, suitcase in hand. But I still had to face my mother.

Mothers are wonderful creatures. There's nobody in

the world like a mother.

She had heard the fight in the kitchen but didn't show herself. My mother was a very smart lady and stayed clear whenever my father and I had a conflict.

This time she knew I was going against my father's will, and she didn't need to wade into it. It was just between him and me. "Where are you going?" she asked when I came marching downstairs with my little suitcase. She had heard me sobbing upstairs on the floor.

"Well, as I told you, when I saw that vision, God told me to preach. So I am going out to preach."

"But where are you going?" she wanted to know.

"Now, Mother, it doesn't make any difference where I'm going. But I am going right now."

She began to cry. Mothers can turn it on and off better than anybody else in the world. They can cry when they're happy, cry when they're sad, cry when they don't know which way they are. They're professionals. So, she began to cry.

I said, "Now, you cried for years because I wasn't saved. You prayed for years that I'd be a preacher. Now I'm going to do it, and you're still crying."

"Oh," she said, "it's tears of joy. Where should I write you?"

"You don't write me," I answered. "I'll write you and tell you where I am. But I have something to tell you. I will not be back. I am going to stay out there as long as I live. I'm going out to stay. So it's good-bye."

I walked out the front door.

I never went back home.

At times my parents came to see me on the road, but it was many years before I went back to the state of Florida; I completely cut my roots.

As soon as I stepped outside the house, there was my old fishing buddy waiting for me.

He said, "Hi, where you going?"

"I'm going out to preach."

He looked me up and down and realized I was serious when he saw my little suitcase.

"Can I go with you?" he asked.

Well, I had never thought of that. "What could you do?" I asked.

He could have asked me the same thing, but he didn't.

"Well, if you do the preaching," he said, "I can do the songs."

"Can you sing?"

"No."

Now he was very nice. He didn't say, "Can you preach?" or I would have had to say "no," too.

Now, if there's anything better than one cabbage, it's two — and we were two green heads.

"Yeah, you can go," I agreed.

Then he said, "You know, my car works."

That's not an unusual statement when you realize that when boys have a car, normally they don't work. I can't remember that his had any fenders, but back in those days boys didn't need fenders on their cars. If it had an engine and a steering wheel and some rubber underneath it, then that was good enough.

He owned a Model T — one of those remarkable cars. It would take three steps forward and two steps back.

"You sure it's going to go at all?" I asked skeptically.

"Oh, yeah. I worked on it myself."

We put more water in that Model T than we did gas. About every ten miles, the engine would get so hot it would just quit. Because we spent all our time babying the car, we didn't have time to worry about what was going to happen to us.

I was going to be a preacher, but I was still full of rebellion and absolute holy terror that God was going to kill me if I didn't obey. I still hated preachers. I didn't want to preach, but God had given me an option: I could do it or die.

I was not filled with compassion for the lost; the Great Commission had no meaning for me. I had no interest in feeding the Lord's sheep or rescuing the perishing. I was rescuing Lester Sumrall. All I cared about was staying alive.

I knew I had to find a pulpit and begin preaching immediately. If I didn't, Almighty God was going to strike me dead.

Like Jonah out of the belly of the whale, I ran to my call with fear in my heart.

If you remember Jonah's story, he absolutely despised the people of Nineveh, even after his humiliating ordeal with the whale. When they fell on their knees before the Lord, he was infuriated because he wanted them to be destroyed.

Expecting to enjoy the view when fire and brimstone fell on them, he built a little hut safely away from the city. When judgment did not come, he prayed an anguished, selfish prayer, asking why God had spared them.

Despite his hatred for an entire nation, God used him — and like the Bible's most reluctant preacher, God set about to use me, too.

Seventeen years old, with no training, no formal preparation, and no guidance from an older preacher, I was set loose on the South.

All I had was a lifetime of hot-headed rebellion and self-centeredness. That made me a fiery young preacher — and an angry one — who had little relationship with God.

I was a know-it-all Jonah with little wisdom to share.

4
Teenage Pulpiteer

After nursing along the old Model-T for a couple of hours, my friend and I were exhausted. We pulled over to the side of the road in north Florida and parked under a persimmon tree loaded with ripe fruit. While Ole Lizzie cooled down, we enjoyed our first meal away from home — free of charge.

Traveling on up the road, I spotted an abandoned country schoolhouse out in the middle of a cotton field.

"Stop the car!" I shouted. "That's the place!"

Somehow in that instant, I knew that was where I wanted to preach. Preaching in some other preacher's church didn't appeal to me. I didn't like churches — and I didn't want any preacher telling me what to do.

I knew where I had to go — out into the cotton fields, the cornfields, and find little backwoods schoolhouses and talk to the country people.

We started going around to nearby farmers' and share-croppers' houses, looking for the owner.

At each door I asked, "Who has the key to the school-house?" I didn't ask who owned the building. I just wanted the key. I was convinced that the Lord had provided my first pulpit.

Finally somebody told me, "That farmer over there. He's in that field plowing."

I started out across the field. As I got closer, I noticed he was dressed not in one pair of overalls but two — one beneath the other — and both were dirty.

"Do you have the key to that schoolhouse over there?" I asked the farmer.

"Yeah," he answered, allowing tobacco juice to dribble out both sides of his mouth.

"Give me that key. I'm going to preach in that schoolhouse," I declared.

He winced, trying to find words to tell me that he'd just as soon not have any young smart-aleck teenager playing preacher in his old school.

Figuring he was just about to turn me down, I quickly said, "I've been sick, and if I don't preach, I'll die."

Then I explained, "God told me that if He was going to allow me to live, I have to preach. Listen, I was dying of tuberculosis in Panama City. God healed me on one condition — that I preach. I haven't preached yet, but I have got to preach, and I have to preach right now. I have to preach tonight. If you don't give me the key to that schoolhouse I'll die of tuberculosis, and you'll be to blame for it."

He stamped his foot and shouted, "No! No!"

I said, "Yes! If you don't let me have that schoolhouse to preach in, then I am going to die, and it will be your fault."

The old farmer's mouth gaped open and the tobacco juice ran down his chin. "Now, Son," he drawled, "I wouldn't want you to die."

"Well, let me borrow that schoolhouse," I begged.

He dug in his pockets and came out with an old key. It was down either in the second pair of overalls, or somewhere below that. Finally, he came out with a key tied on the end of an old greasy string.

"Here it is. Go unlock it," he said reluctantly.

"Do you have a lantern? I need a lantern." There was no electricity out in that cotton patch.

"Oh yeah. My house is over there. Go tell my wife," he said, walking away shaking his head and chuckling under his breath. I didn't mind since he was amused enough to start spreading the word that something really odd was going on in his old schoolhouse.

My friend and I went over and swept up the place and had church that night. Eight farmers showed up.

Why were they there? Because we were the best entertainment in months.

It was 1929, the year the stock market had crashed up in faraway New York City. There was no TV and not that many radios. Nobody could afford to go into town to the nickel movie except for special occasions. The South was already poorer than the rest of the country, but now the Great Depression was blanketing the Deep South with great new hardships.

After a long day in the fields, with all the chores done, we were almost as good as a traveling juggler, a dog-and-pony act, or a magic show. These rough, good-ol'-boys showed up to hear me just as they would have done for a snake-oil salesman. They were willing to hear my pitch, but they weren't intending to buy anything.

Not a single woman came. Just men. They came in talking loudly and cussing, obviously unaware that this was supposed to be church. None of them had washed before they came; they were all dirty.

There were no pews in the schoolhouse — just rather crude wooden desks. Unaccustomed to such seating, the men scooted down in their desks until all I could see was their noses and bald heads peeking up at me. From my vantage point, they looked like creatures from outer space.

To make matters worse, they were all chewing and spitting tobacco. It would hit the wall — kawoomp. Having been reared in the city, this was a little too much for me. I didn't like what I had gotten into.

I wondered if I shouldn't have taken that beautiful coffin and died. This was almost worse than death.

I was pretty discouraged.

"Go ahead and lead the song service," I told my friend. Having been forced to attend lots of church revivals, we at least knew the proper order of service.

Four minutes later, he turned to me and said, "I'm finished." Since he couldn't sing and neither could the eight men, he gave it back to me.

As I stared out at them, I realized I didn't know what I was going to say. So, drawing on years of hearing church testimonials, I figured I would tell them all about my tuberculosis, my vision of the coffin, and the big Bible.

I said, "Well, I'll tell you. I was a bad boy."

They all laughed.

"I stole things, and I'm sorry," I declared in total seriousness.

They roared with laughter.

"I got sick with tuberculosis."

They howled.

"You're the craziest bunch of men," I told them. "You've laughed at everything I've said. Just laughed out loud."

They got a little more serious, and I told them my full testimony. Still they laughed, and sometimes they would even hit the desk with their hands. This must have been the first side show they'd had in that area for a long time.

I was so mad when I got through. I said, "Go on home." I didn't tell them to come back or anything.

Under my breath I said, "I hope all of you go to hell."

Since we had no place to stay, my friend and I went home with one of the men.

When I finally got off by myself, I tried to figure out what to do next.

"Man, man, man," I muttered to myself. "I think it would have been better to have died than to get in a mess like this. You know they won't come back. I told them to go home. They won't come back. So tomorrow night when there's nobody there, I'll tell the Lord, 'Now, You see Lord, I did a good job. Finished my work. Now I'm going back home and go to work and be a businessman.' "

All night and all the next day, I was saying, "Man, I finished that thing off last night. I really did."

But when I got to church the next evening, there were forty people there, including some ladies and a couple of kids.

I said to myself, *Now, wait a minute. How'd this happen?*

Those eight men had told everybody they knew about the kid trying to hold a revival. "But this is no revival," they said. "The biggest liar that every came through these parts has arrived. You've never heard lies like this guy can tell. Come out and hear him." So they came to hear a liar, not a preacher.

When I saw all those people, I knew I had to do something. I knew my songleader wasn't going to take up much time. He might have been up there six minutes this time, then he quickly handed the service over to me. But he did lead the prayer.

I didn't know what to do, so I did the same thing as the night before. I said, "I'll tell you why I'm here. I was born in a half-Christian home, half-baked. My mother was a Christian, my father . . . ."

But they were roaring with laughter again.

Blast it, I thought, *I've got a bunch of laughers again. Spitting tobacco juice and laughing at me.* I was miserable.

I told the whole story, and they'd talk out loud. They'd say, "See, I told you about this liar. Did you hear that?"

I was still preaching, and they were talking among themselves. So I said, "Well, that is just terrible."

I didn't give an altar call. I didn't want anybody to get saved. I was too upset at them.

The next morning, the farmer we were staying with

said, "Young man, if you don't work, you don't eat. If you are going to stay here for a few days, you're going to feed the hogs."

"Feed the hogs?" I exclaimed.

"Yeah. If you don't work, you don't eat."

"But," I protested, "preaching is working."

"No, what you're doing is not working," he laughed.

Well, he was about right.

I had never fed any hogs. I had lived in the city all my life. We had ham and bacon on the table, but we had never had it in the pigpen.

In fact, I had never even seen a hog slop bucket. Slop is the stuff that today we pour down our garbage disposals. It's the spoiled lettuce, the tops of carrots, and the eggs that rotted, and the bread that molded. It's the guts of the chickens.

It was gathered daily in buckets left in the kitchen — the spoiled milk, the rancid grease, the wormy pieces of apples, the meatloaf that nobody ate, and the stew that had gone bad. After sitting in the kitchen all day and night, this bucket full of awful mess stank to high heaven.

The pigpen was several hundred feet from the house. As I carried those heavy buckets, the wretched stuff sloshed over onto my clothes and into my shoes.

I didn't even know how to call hogs, so I just bellowed at them and they came. As they grunted and snorted and wallowed in their stench, tears ran down my cheeks.

Those hogs were the most ungrateful things in the world. They were terrible. They were just simply awful. The way they would eat was just so disgusting. They would just gobble it all up as though they weren't going to get enough. I would just get madder all the time.

Beside the pigpen was a cornfield. I went and laid down in it and said, "God, I must be the prodigal son. I must be. I'm in the pigpen, and I'm away from home. I must be the prodigal. You must be paying me back for my sins that I did when I was at home."

God began to speak to me.

He said, "If you will be faithful in little things I will give you bigger things to take care of. If you won't quit and don't stop, if you'll march forward, I'll let you touch many people by My power — and you will bless multitudes of people."

I got up out of the cornfield by the pigpen, went back into the house, and took a bath so I wouldn't stink like the pigs. Then I began to study the Bible, to find out how to preach to those people.

Well, the next night God began to save those people.

It had to be God because I would say, "If you want to get saved kneel down at the altar." Then I'd pick up my Bible and go out the side door, and I was gone. I didn't stay to see what they did. That wasn't part of the deal. My deal was to preach, and I had nothing to do with getting people saved. So if they got saved, they had to want to.

People kept coming — more every night.

As I worked for that farmer, I prayed. In the morning before sunrise, I read my Bible, and I cried out to the Lord to show me what to say to those people — and He gave me the words.

Believe me, it was God — not me. I really disliked those people — but after six weeks, a whole gang had been saved.

They came to me and kept saying, "Water baptism. Water baptism."

I said, "Okay. Sure." But I had never baptized anybody.

"You're a preacher. You baptize us."

"Oh, sure. Yeah." I kept stalling.

They said, "We've got a creek close by. We'll go down and get baptized."

So, on a Sunday afternoon here we went, two or three hundred people.

"How many want to be baptized?" I asked.

There were sixty-seven.

Not knowing what I was doing, I backed off into the river.

That day I learned what every experienced preacher knows: Don't ever back off into a river. If the man in front of the preacher has water up to his waist and the preacher has it up to his neck, the preacher's at a serious disadvantage. I didn't know that so I did what seemed best and turned to face the people on the river bank. I should have let the candidate for baptism face the people.

The first farmer who came down had a big pair of overalls on — just like the rest of them. This man must have weighed 350 pounds and stood 6-foot-4. I was 5-foot-8. When he walked down in that water, I couldn't see the sun anymore. All I could see was a looming hulk, like Goliath.

"Dear God, why did he come first?" I asked. "The first one I've ever baptized, and he blacks out the sun."

He got down in front of me, and I said, "You better help me."

"Yeah, Little Preacher, I'll help you," he replied. I didn't weigh a hundred pounds yet.

I whispered to him, "When I do this in the name of the Father, you squat."

He said, "I'll do anything you tell me to, Little Preacher."

I got hold of the back of his overalls, and I put my hand up in front. When I put my arm across him, it was like trying to hold a cow. I couldn't reach all the way over him.

I said, "According to your acceptance of Jesus Christ as your Lord and Saviour and because you have given up your life as a sinner and because you have positively accepted Jesus Christ as your Saviour, upon the authority of the Word of God, the Bible, I do, here and now, before this group of witnesses to your water baptism, obey the words of Matthew's Gospel. I now baptize you in the name of the Father and of the Son and of the Holy Ghost."

I began to pull and I went down first. As I started to pull, he got on top of me and I went to the bottom. He helped all he could, but he was just too big.

When I came up the farmers on the bank were actually rolling in the sand with laughter. They thought it was the funniest thing they had ever seen.

Actually, it *was* the funniest thing they had ever seen.

"Next, please." I said, gathering as much dignity as I could.

Then, I told Goliath, "You stand by to help me."

I wanted to make sure that I didn't go under any more.

The rest of the group were smaller, and we baptized all sixty-seven.

Two missionaries to Africa and one of the finest pastors in this country resulted from those first revival meetings, and people have worshipped in that place from then until this very day.

From there, I went from little country schoolhouse to little country schoolhouse. In fact, I don't remember meeting a single preacher or seeing a single church.

I just stayed in the country where I belonged. Country people will endure you when others won't. They'll keep coming back when you wonder why.

My songleader began to get where he could sing and really lead worship. He got better. They say I got better, too. I don't know, because I sure wasn't a happy preacher. I suppose you could say I was a most unhappy, unthankful, and ungrateful preacher.

My heart was still hard. I was preaching out of obedience with no compassion for the people. I didn't care if they got saved or not.

Irritated and agitated on the inside and not wanting to preach, I would sometimes tell the people, "I don't want you to think I like you, because I don't. Really, I didn't want to die of tuberculosis, but God said I could live if I would preach. I am preaching so I won't die. I hope all of you understand that. If you do, then you'll know why I act like I do."

Maybe that's the reason sometimes the total offering

I got was twenty-six cents in one week. Of course, the Depression was gripping America.

Twenty-six pennies. Nobody gave a nickel. A nickel was a lot of money.

We had to live so, when I got an offering like that, I got right up and asked the congregation, "How many of you have chickens at your house?" They would all raise their hands.

I would say, "There will be a coop right outside the door tomorrow night. Every one of you bring me a chicken or two and put it in that coop."

By the next night, I had three coops of chickens. Then I took them over to the wholesale poultry house and came back with money in my pocket.

At least I had some money to live on, but my sermons continued to be terrible. I told Bible stories and quoted Scripture. I went through the motions. I had heard enough preachers over the years to know how to craft a sermon. The only problem was that I had no anointing. Instead, I fell back on gimmicks.

To illustrate my sermons, I would have people from the congregation put on costumes and act out the Bible characters I was describing in my sermons. That always worked. If old Mrs. Jones was going to be Queen Esther that night, you can bet that her kids, grandkids, great-grandkids, nieces, neighbors, and garden club members were all there to see her in her glory.

Because I drew good crowds, I began getting invitations to minister in real churches instead of schoolhouses. From one rural community to another, I preached across northern Florida, then into Alabama, Mississippi, and Tennessee.

My preaching became more and more enthusiastic because that seemed to be what people liked. I stalked the devil around the church, shouting at sinners to repent. I would run down the aisle and shake my finger in the faces of sinners and describe the burning lake of brimstone waiting for them.

By the end of my sermon, my voice would be hoarse and my body drenched with perspiration — but it was all theatrics.

I am ashamed to say that I didn't love those people at all. I was just living up to my end of the deal with God. I was preaching like He had said I had to — and I hated it.

I took out my resentment on sinners. I roared my "righteous" fury at unrepentant adulterers and tobacco chewers and greedy bankers.

Why was I so angry?

I gave God my obedience, but I was no cheerful giver. Sure, I had read 2 Corinthians 9:7. It proclaims that we should give as our hearts tell us and not with pain or reluctance or with a sense of necessity.

Yet, I only used that verse to pound people with guilt, saying they should bring me chickens and offerings and be cheerful about it. I could not see that verse 7 is preceded by verse 5, which says that gifts to God's people should be a result of joy and willingness, not squeezed out of them by preached extortion.

After all, deep inside, I believed the Almighty Father was blackmailing me. So, I squeezed the emotions and guilt and doubts of my listeners and refused to surrender my own heart.

I preached like a raving madman. People flocked down the aisles and wept at the altar.

Was God pleased? Well, He used me, despite my human, youthful rebellion.

Hundreds and thousands of souls were saved.

What was so wrong with my message? After all, John the Baptist was angry much of the time — and it cost him his head. The apostle Peter had a real problem with not only cowardice but anger. Jesus nicknamed the apostles James and John, "the sons of thunder."

If you read the Old Testament, there are many examples of raging men of God thundering terrible warnings upon Judah and Israel if they did not return to the Lord.

In 2 Kings 2:23-24, a gang of "little children" mocked the prophet Elisha, making fun of his bald head. The Bible says "he turned back and looked on them and cursed them in the name of the Lord." Suddenly, two bears burst out of the woods and killed forty-two of them.

Listen to the words of the prophet Hosea, who in obedience to God married a harlot as a dramatic example to God's people of their terrible unfaithfulness: "Give them, O Lord: what wilt thou give? give them a miscarrying womb and dry breasts. All their wickedness is in Gilgal; for there I hated them" (Hos. 9:14-15).

The fourth chapter of Jonah details how furious Jonah was when God did not destroy Nineveh. In spite of all these examples, the Bible is also filled with repeated cautions about anger.

The writings of Old Testament prophets reflect their deep, heart-felt compassion. Jeremiah wept and pleaded with the Lord to withhold His punishment of His faithless people.

The books of Nahum, Habukkuk, and Malachi start off describing "the burden" these prophets felt for God's children.

Isaiah, throughout his prophecies, lovingly pleaded with the people of his day to return to their loving God.

I lacked the ancient prophets' compassion. I only thundered. I didn't have any love for the people.

I was honest about it, though — too honest.

I would say, "You guys stink. I can smell you clear up here. You didn't take a bath before you came. I'm from New Orleans. We take baths down there."

You know an eighteen-year-old will say anything.

One night in the middle of a sermon, I demanded of a young woman, "Do you want to go to heaven?"

She shook her head no.

Furious, I spat at her, "Then you go to hell."

She fainted.

5

Blood on My Hands

While we were having a revival meeting in a schoolhouse in Tennessee, I was sitting on the side watching my friend lead the people in singing. After months of practice, he had really improved and everybody was clapping and praising the Lord.

Suddenly, with my eyes wide open, I didn't see him. I didn't see the people. I saw the world.

Before me I saw all the people of the entire world — people of every color brightly dressed in their native costumes. I was impressed with how beautiful they were as they walked down a very long and wide highway leading away from me.

I saw the Japanese in their colorful kimonos. I saw the Mongolians, rough, tough, and bearded — it was almost scary. I saw all different kinds of Chinese. Some were elegantly dressed. I saw South Sea islanders, naked and mean.

I saw people from South America, Africa, India, and Europe. I saw the world. It was real as my flesh. I saw people from every nation.

Millions and millions of people were all walking on

a highway. But they weren't walking, they stepped with a little trot. I watched them with interest. It was exciting!

In my vision, God picked me up, and away I went over the top of the people to the end of their highway. I could look down.

God said, "That is the road of life."

At the end of their highway was a raging, bottomless inferno. Flames leaped up out of what looked like a blazing volcano.

The vast procession of people marched to the edge, then fell screaming into the eternal flames. As they neared the pit and saw their fate, they struggled in vain, trying to push back against the unrelenting march of those behind them. The great surging river of humanity swept them over into the abyss.

Over the edge they went, a hundred thousand at a time. As they would go down into it screaming, yelling, crying, tearing their hair, scratching their faces, I lost my breath, "God . . . God . . . God," I gasped. I saw the world going to hell.

God opened my ears to hear the screams of damned souls sinking into hell. As He brought me nearer I could see men and women of all nations, their faces distorted with terror, their hands flailing wildly, clawing at the air.

God spoke to me out of the chaos: "You are responsible for these who are lost."

"Me Lord?" I protested. "I do not know these people. I have never been to Japan or China or India. I'm not to blame!"

God's voice was tender yet firm as He spoke again: "When I say unto the wicked, 'Thou shalt surely die,' and thou givest him not warning, nor speakest to warn the wicked from his wicked way, to save his life; the same wicked man shall die in his iniquity, but his blood will I require at your hand."

That was the shortest sermon I had ever heard and the most frightening. It was preached to me by God himself. Not until a week later did I discover that He had quoted a passage from the Bible — Ezekiel 3:18.

As I continued to stare, the people tried to back up, but the pressure from behind pushed them on — and into hell they would fall, catapulted into the air screaming and crying.

They had not thought about eternity until they got there. Isn't that amazing?

I looked at it and I observed this scene for I don't know how long.

What had God spoken to me? "You are to blame for it," He had said.

"Not me," I had declared. "I was born in New Orleans, Louisiana. I've lived in Mobile, Alabama and Panama City, Florida. I have never been abroad. I am not to blame!"

I heard His answer ringing in my ears: "If the ungodly commits his ungodly deeds and he dies in his ungodliness and you don't warn him of his ungodliness I will cause his blood to be upon your hands."

Suddenly I saw blood running through my fingers. The blood of the nations.

That is why today I speak to millions of people — because God put a burden in my heart for the nations.

God knows how to make a missionary when He wants to.

I saw the blood and said, "God, what can I do?"

He said, "What the Word says. Tell them, reprove them, rebuke them, the nations."

"The nations?" I asked.

"The nations, you saw them go to hell. My Word says, 'If the ungodly dies in his ungodliness and you don't warn him of his ungodliness, I will demand his blood at your hands.' "

"God, why don't You tell everybody, not just me?"

"I have. It is in My Book." He said, "You are going to be judged by the Book. If you go to court and tell the judge that you didn't know you were wrong he will just tell you that ignorance of the law is no excuse. You had better know the laws of the land. In the same way, you had better know the laws of eternity."

I said, "Okay, Lord, what should I do?"

At that moment I woke. Suddenly the vision was over. I was still trembling.

Opening my eyes, I saw that the meeting house was dark and I was alone.

I couldn't tell you if I was there for an hour, an hour and a half, two hours, I don't know. I never had enough courage to ask the people if they had tried to shake me. In fact, I never talked to anybody about that meeting. I was too ashamed.

After all, I was only nineteen years old. I don't know if they thought I went to sleep and they did it as a joke or what. But all those people went home and took the lantern with them.

When I came back to my natural self, I was in a dark little school building all alone.

I said to myself, *I'm back in Tennessee. I have seen the whole world — but hell, Lester, hell is real. You had better stay out of there. You saw it. Don't say that you don't know anything about it. You saw it! You saw the people who were going to hell. You saw it! Their blood is on your hands unless you warn them of their evilness.*

I cried out, "God," as I fell to the floor.

Little country schoolhouses are not very clean. The people bring in mud, and they don't wash it off. They just sweep off the top.

I went down on the floor, and in those days I was a very elegant young man. I would preach in a white tie, white shirts, white trousers, white socks, and white shoes. I was the white young preacher from Florida, but without hesitating, I stretched out on that dirty floor.

I began to weep and to cry, asking forgiveness of my sins. Asking forgiveness for the way I had treated people.

Asking forgiveness for the times I hadn't given an altar call in my services when I should have. Asking forgiveness because I hadn't gotten down and prayed with people seeking salvation.

I cleansed my spirit and my soul.

Then I began to pray. "God, all those people from Japan. Oh, God, all those people from China. Oh, God, all those people from India. Lord!"

That was the first time in my life that I had prayed for the nations of the world.

I began to hurt all over. My body started to sweat. The sweat mingled with that mud.

All night long, until eight o'clock the next morning, I cried; I prayed; I travailed.

Maybe you don't know what the word travail means, but Jesus travailed in the Garden of Gethsemane. He travailed so deeply that blood pressed itself through the skin and ran down His face. It burst the blood vessels and came out. He knew what travail was.

That has happened only three or four times in my whole life. But I have travailed until I almost died, and I felt as if I might die that night.

The next morning at eight o'clock, the light was coming through the shutters of the little school building.

I got up. I never had been such a mess. My white clothes were red from the mud. I had mud in my hair and on my face. I had prayed on my knees; I had prayed on my back; and I had prayed on my stomach. I had prayed every way possible. I looked like a hog that had been in a pigpen. It was awful.

I said to myself, *I've got to slip away and get clean. I can't let anybody ever see this.*

Nobody saw me. God made it possible.

I slipped over to the place where I was staying, removed those stained clothes, and bathed.

When I came out, people asked me, "Did you stay in church all night?"

"Yes," I answered.

"Something happened to you, didn't it?"

"Yes."

I had prostrated myself on that wooden floor and remained there all night agonizing before the Lord. "Oh, God," I had implored, "forgive me. Forgive me for not loving the least, the last, and the lost of the world."

When I walked out of that little building the next morning, I was a new man. Something had matured in my heart and my soul. I had been set apart and given a call.

God had given me a compassion for the lost that I had never felt before. He also filled me with an urgency that has remained strong even to this day.

Every day, millions die and go straight to hell.

It was several years before I ever told anyone what I had seen that night.

The next evening, the people wanted to know what had happened and I said, "God and I talked together." That was all that I would say.

How could I proclaim that out of the poverty-stricken Old Confederacy, out of the Great Depression, out of a little country schoolhouse, here was a skinny teenager who said he was being called to a world ministry? How could I explain that the Lord had put the blood of the lost millions on my hands?

That same night, my buddy, the songleader, saw a little Tennessee girl by the name of Lily Belle. He fell so crazy in love with her that I thought he'd gone insane.

Ten days later, he found a Justice of the Peace and married her, leaving me behind without even saying "Good-bye." In fact, he didn't even tell me he was getting married. Next I heard, he'd gone back to Florida.

I never saw him again. I can't even remember his name.

I was now on my own.

6

Ordained by God

If Moses had waited for a committee to get together, he would never have delivered the children of Israel. Sometimes God has to do a thing through a single person, not a panel of experts.

The call of God can make you independent.

After my buddy left me, I wondered how I was going to go around the world on my own. I had so little money.

One day as I was praying, God spoke to me and said, "Read John 15:16. It says, 'You have not chosen me, but I have chosen you.' "

As I read that I thought, *I'm sure glad to hear that.*

In every crisis of my life, God has spoken to me through His Word. Not through a little box of cards with Bible promises and not by just letting the Bible fall open, but every time the Lord has said, "This is your verse, for this moment."

This time He said, "I have anointed you."

The word anoint means "to ordain. To set apart, to dedicate."

God said, "I have set you apart. I have dedicated you. I am sending you forth. I have ordained you to do this."

No man can stop you when God ordains you to do a thing. When God says "I am doing it and you're the instrument," you'll do it, no matter how big or broad it is.

I went back and reread John 15:16, "You have not chosen me, I have chosen you and ordained you that you should go."

"Oh! So that's what I'm doing," I realized even though I was still in rural Tennessee. "I'm not sitting in a rocking chair. I'm on my way right now around the world. My suitcase is right here with me and I'm in movement."

I was willing. I just didn't know how it was going to happen.

God said, "That's the way I like it." He saw in me something that others did not see.

He said, "You haven't chosen me. I've chosen you — and ordained you."

Ordained me?

I was called a freelancer. I wasn't ordained or licensed, I was just a teenage preacher obeying God.

After a while my crusades attracted the attention of church officials. Every time I held a crusade, I would leave behind a brand-new church.

I would stay several weeks, and the farmers would say, "Let's build a church." They usually had enough wood in their sheds to do the job.

I'd say, "Sure," and we would all get together and put up a building. Then I'd write a letter to the denomination in which I had been raised and ask them to send a pastor.

After eight or nine times, the church officials began to ask questions. "Who is this young preacher establishing all these new churches?"

I had no official position in the denomination. I just knew the people needed leadership.

By the time I got up to Tennessee, the denomination sent some representatives down to talk to me. "We'd like to license you," they said.

"Well, what's that?" I asked.

"We'll give you a piece of paper that you can hang on the wall. It will get you into hospitals and prisons."

I didn't have any walls, and I wasn't having any trouble getting into prisons or hospitals.

"I've preached in them already," I said. "I just don't quite see what you're doing."

"It would give you recognition."

I said, "Well, I think I might need that. All right, let's do it." So, the Tennessee state conference licensed me to preach. Actually, I didn't like it very much, but I accepted it because I thought it was the thing to do.

I kept going on further north — to Blytheville, Arkansas, then Fayetteville, Eureka Springs, and Fort Smith — to hold meetings. Then one day several teen-agers came to see me. They were just kids, none of them even twenty years old. For that matter, I wasn't either.

"Would you come to the little town of Green Forest, Arkansas and preach?" they asked. "We need a revival there."

Impressed with their sincerity, I said, "I'll go anywhere and preach."

"We have a community church building that belongs to everybody, " they said. "You can preach there."

So I said, "All right."

When I got there, sure enough they had a nice community church building made of Ozark mountain stone. It had no lock on the door. Whenever someone wanted to use the building, they just walked in and started preaching.

I went around town and talked to people on the square and put up lots of signs and announced all around that I was going to preach.

We had a real good turn-out although the kids who had invited me weren't much help. They came to the services, but they didn't do anything to spread the word.

The Lord sent the people. They just poured in.

After three or four nights of large crowds, a couple of

tough-looking characters, twice my size, came in just before the evening service was to begin and said, "Well, you've had your time. You have to get out. We're going to take the pulpit here tonight."

I was still a teenager — people were still calling me "Little Preacher." I guess those hooligans thought I was just some sissified seminary graduate who would just apologize and leave. They had no idea that they were talking to a former delinquent, ex-brawler, and the son of a prayer warrior.

"You and who else?" I asked. "You're not taking the pulpit. I'm preaching a revival."

"We'll take over from here," they said. "This church belongs to everybody,"

"That means me," I said, "so you get out."

"Look, you, we've been preaching here for years. You're not going to take our people."

"That's all finished. I'm here for a crusade. I'm not here just for a day or two."

"This place belongs to the public," they said. "We're the public. You have to get out."

"Well, now," I said, "I'm not going to get out. You've had it before, and I'm going to have it now."

When they saw that I couldn't be bullied, they said, "We'll see about that. We'll see you tomorrow."

The next day, I did two things. First, I went to see the sheriff. He had been in the services almost every night, so I knew him. "Man, they think they're going to throw me out of the pulpit tonight. Could you stop them?" I asked.

He said, "Oh, yeah, I know those guys, too. If they do anything to you, I'll just put them in jail for the night."

Then I went to see the old man who had built the community church for the town. He lived out in the country and was up in his eighties.

"I'm preaching at the church that you built," I said as I shook his hand. "Have you heard about our crusade?"

"Yes, I have," he said. "I'm so glad for it."

"The wrong people have been using it," I told him. "There's a bunch of hooligans who think they own the place. I don't like what I've seen of them or what I've heard about their false doctrine. It seems to me that it would be a good thing for them to get out of there."

"You're right. I don't want those kind of people using my building. But what can I do?" he asked.

"I think you should give that church to me," I answered.

Now, that was pretty brash — but I was not at all surprised when he said, "Why not?"

We sat down together, and he signed a paper, giving the property to me. I also promised that I would assign it to a legitimate church group so that it wouldn't be my personal property.

That afternoon, I went to the church building in case those characters showed up early. Sure enough long before the service was to begin, they came in to take the church away from me. But, I stood my ground behind the pulpit.

They argued and tried to intimidate me, but as the people came in, I was still there holding my ground. News of what was supposed to happen had gotten around town, and the building was packed, inside and outside. Most folks thought we were going to have a fist fight.

We sang a little bit, then I told the crowd, "I have some wonderful news for you. One is that the sheriff is sitting over there and, if anyone disturbs this meeting tonight, he's going to put you in jail at least for one night."

Then I pulled out this sheet of paper and said, "And, by the way, I went to see the gentleman who owns this building. He gave it to me today and signed this paper. I'm going to register it tomorrow morning in the courthouse, and this church will belong to the denomination that I have attended since I was a little child."

Those big fellows got so mad they didn't know what to do. "Why didn't we do that before he came?" they asked each other.

They left, and we never saw them again.

I stayed another six or seven months and established the people in the Word. I preached how they should love God, serve Him, and live right. When I thought the congregation had a solid group of believers, I contacted the state conference and they sent a pastor.

The news went throughout Arkansas, "Hey, here's a guy who is really something else. He goes and takes churches away from people and gives them to us."

The denominational church officials were pretty impressed with me, and one of the executive presbyters told me, "I think we should ordain you." Remember, I wasn't nineteen yet.

I said, "I've already got one sheet of paper, but I've never hung it up yet anywhere."

They said, "Oh, that's not as important as this one."

I said, "Well, I guess you know what's best. What do I have to do?"

They said, "You've already done it. You brought that stone church into our denomination, and we had no church at all in that area. We are very proud of you. A man who can do that ought to be ordained."

Although I couldn't see the relationship exactly, I agreed, "Well, I'll let you do whatever you want to."

When I went to the district council meetings in North Little Rock, the head man in the denomination came to officiate. After he preached a little, he said he was going to ordain us.

There were about thirty or forty young preachers stretched clear across the front of the church.

As this important official came by, he patted each candidate on the head and said, "Op," and then went to the next one and said, "Op."

After he got down the way a little bit, I turned to the man on my right and I said, "Did you get anything?"

"No, I didn't get anything," he answered.

"Well, I didn't get anything either."

I turned to the man on my left and I said, "Did you get anything?"

He said, "No."

"Well, what's this thing all about then, if you don't get anything?" I asked.

About an hour later, after the service was over, I was standing out in the churchyard when the top official, a very austere type of person, came briskly walking by.

I stopped him and said, "How do you do, sir?"

He did shake my hand.

I said, "I'm Lester Sumrall."

He said, "Oh?"

"You ordained me."

"Oh," he replied and turned around and walked off.

I was very disappointed.

A teenage boy doesn't know much, but I knew that was wrong. My feelings were hurt. The man who ordained me an hour before didn't know me or anything about me.

I thought, *This thing doesn't work right, does it?*

When I was only eighteen and a half, I decided that a man should be ordained in his own church by his own pastor — by the ones who brought him into the ministry, who loved him and succored him and picked him up when he fell.

I was headed for trouble with that denomination before I even got started, but at least I got ordained and had a second sheet of paper.

Almost everybody has been ordained by somebody, but the Lord had said to me, "I have ordained you."

God not only chooses us, He gives us the force and the power to follow our calling. No church or denomination can do that.

When Jesus empowers the one He calls and ordains, that person knows it! You feel the holy anointing. It comes upon you, and you know you've moved into the realm of the supernatural. You know you have come under the holy anointing of the One who has chosen you — not just ordained you but anointed you for service.

Remember, the Lord had told me, "You have not chosen me, I have chosen you."

It's His choice.

7

Shotgun Revival

Not long after my official ordination, my little sister, Leona, joined me. It was good to have a songleader again. Her anointed guitar playing and singing added a sweet spirit to the services.

It was a good time in my life.

I was becoming a real preacher. Sometimes, I would even go out into the aisles and personally invite people to come to the altar.

One night, I saw a man who looked very sad. I went over to him and said, "Come give your heart to God."

"Little Preacher," he replied, "I want to and, if you'll give me until next Sunday night, I swear I'll go to the altar."

"You know, I've heard that before. What if you don't live until Sunday night?"

"Oh, I'll live."

"Why don't you want to come tonight?" I asked

"Well," he said — right there in the service — but with his voice low so that only I could hear him. "I'll tell you. There's a man running around with my wife, and they are sleeping together here in town. I have vowed to kill him."

He pulled his coat back and said, "See, I carry this gun with me all the time to kill him, but since talking to you and hearing you, I'm not going to kill him. But I do need to ask his forgiveness and tell him he can have the woman if he wants her."

I am told that he looked for that man that week, but the other guy stayed out of his way.

The next Sunday night, I had been preaching about ten minutes when, from one side of the church, a man walked in. At that moment, the man whose wife had been cheating jumped up.

Both men grabbed for their guns. The adulterer was a little faster. Bang, bang, bang, he pumped the wronged husband full of lead — dead, right there, inside the church.

The sheriff leaped up, as did everybody in the church. The killer didn't run at all. He just stood over to the side and waited for the sheriff to arrest him.

A great commotion broke out in the church. Children screamed. Men grabbed their daughters. Women fainted. But I commanded the crowd to return to their seats, "Sit down! I command you to sit down!"

Stunned they all sat down. Immediately, I gave an altar call. "That man lying dead on the floor promised me he'd come to God tonight. You have seen with your own eyes that he got within fifty feet of salvation, but went to hell."

People streamed to the altar.

While they were wrapping his body up and taking him out and washing up the blood, almost the entire town got saved.

The next day, word of what had happened spread like wildfire. We had crowds for weeks. You couldn't get in the building unless you arrived an hour early.

Later, during a meeting in Charleston, Arkansas, a young ruffian was standing outside the church with his rowdy buddies, watching the service through the window. Suddenly, this young thug noticed that his sister had responded to the altar call. He burst into our service and, grabbing his sister, pulled her up from her knees, threw her across his shoulder, and carried her outside where in front of his drunken friends, he commanded her never to go back to church.

A few days later, he was plowing in the field and a bolt of lightning struck him dead.

When the time came to close that revival, my sister and I were packing the car. A crowd gathered and begged us to stay. They laid down on the car and wept, crying out, "You can't leave yet. We have loved ones who aren't saved and are going to hell."

We unpacked the car, and the revival continued for another week.

Another time, a man came to church to kill me.

The night before, in the middle of my sermon, tires had screeched outside the church. Everyone jumped to their feet.

"A man has been killed!" someone yelled. Others yelled that a drunk had staggered out in front of a car and been killed instantly.

Immediately I gave the altar call, challenging the crowd not to suffer the fate of a man who'd had the chance that night to come to church or go get drunk at the bar across the street. I shouted that now he was dead and in hell.

Amid the commotion outside and the sound of a police siren filling the air, the prayer rail filled to capacity.

The next morning, four young men banged on my door and demanded that I come out. When I stepped onto the porch, one of them shoved me and another one yelled, "We're going to kill you, Little Preacher."

"Why?" I stuttered.

"Our daddy wasn't drunk. He got run over last night, and you said he was a drunk."

"I'm sorry," I apologized. "I didn't mean any offense."

"Well, offense is taken," yelled another one of the boys. "You said he's burning in hell."

"I'm sorry," I repeated.

As the boys jumped in their car and left, I was shaken. I asked the Lord to forgive me — and protect me.

I arrived at the church an hour early and was startled to find that folks were already there. The mood was ugly, too.

"I'm going home," the pastor whispered to me. "You could get killed here tonight." He left.

"What are you going to do?" people asked. "Those boys are coming to kill you tonight. You talked against their dead father. They've vowed to shoot you dead if you step into that pulpit."

"In that case," I said, "let them kill me."

I got up and started the song service, but cut the songs short before it was time for Leona to get up. As I began to preach, people kept interrupting my sermon to warn me that my life was in danger and I should get out of town.

Irritated, I shouted, "Listen, God is with me! Anybody here who pulls a trigger against me will die. God himself will strike him dead. I dare you to do it. Quit stalling around. If you're going to do it, stand up right now and do it."

The fear of the Lord came upon those people. They sat in shocked stillness. I finished my sermon and opened the altar.

As was my style back then, I scanned the crowd for people the Lord would show me needed to get saved. I called out to a grim-faced young man sitting on the aisle, "Young man, God is talking to you tonight!"

"How do you know?" he snarled, standing.

The crowd gasped. People scattered.

"God tells me He is talking to you."

"Don't you know who I am?"

"No, I don't, but God does."

"It was my daddy you lied about," he shouted. "I

came here to kill you." With that, he pulled out a gun.

I had not recognized him as one of the boys on my porch until that very moment.

"Listen, I don't know where your daddy is," I told him. "I shouldn't have said that without checking whether it was true. But I'll tell you this, I know you are going to hell for your sins if you don't get right with God."

He began to weep bitterly. I walked down the aisle and knelt with him.

Instead of killing me, he gave his heart to Jesus. What a glorious night! Many souls were saved — including his.

Despite such occasional danger, it was good to have Leona helping me. I adored my little sister. We had grown up together. The older kids had all grown up and gotten married by the time I was ten, so she and I were playmates when we were little.

Shortly after I became a preacher, she came to hear me. During an altar call, I went back and touched her on the shoulder and said, "Leona, come on down and give your heart to Jesus."

She walked the aisle and knelt at the altar, giving her life to Jesus. It was so good to have her assisting me with the crusades. I know that many times, sinners came just so they could hear her sing.

Having her along also kept local girls from pestering me. Leona wouldn't let them come around.

She traveled with me for about a year, then went out on her own, preaching and holding meetings. While in Louisiana she decided to build a church even before she had anybody saved. My mother, who was working with my sister, asked different people in town to give them the materials. Before long, they had their own church building.

People came from all over to see the two of them, a woman and a young girl holding gospel meetings. The whole city just loved them.

Many people were saved, and a good, strong church

was established.

At a meeting in Baton Rouge, Louisiana, a young man who was stationed at a military base near where Leona was holding a crusade, came to the meeting one night. In fact, he kept coming to see her, even when she went up into Indiana to hold another crusade. They fell in love and eventually got married.

I always marveled at Leona's powerful preaching. She had something I knew I needed.

Although I had been raised among Pentecostals, I had never experienced the in-filling of the Holy Spirit. I had obeyed the Lord's command to go preach. I had learned to love the lost, but I lacked the power of the Spirit in my life.

As my reputation spread as the Little Preacher, the bold teenage evangelist, I was troubled by a deep feeling of emptiness.

I wanted to have the Holy Spirit living within me. I had seen His great power during all those years of being dragged to my mother's church services. Desperately, I sought the in-filling.

Often, I would preach about the Holy Spirit, but it was not from my own experience, just from what I had heard and seen, as well as what the Bible teaches.

From the pulpit, I challenged others to seek the blessing. Many came down to the altar and received it, but people would say, "That Little Preacher has no right to preach about the Holy Ghost. He doesn't even have the Baptism himself."

They were absolutely right. I would tell the congregation that they should seek the in-filling, then I would join them at the altar seeking it myself.

After other people had received the Holy Spirit following my altar calls, sometimes folks would gather around me and pray that I would receive the in-filling. I can remember so many times that they tried to "pray the preacher through."

They would lay their hands on me and instruct me to repeat nonsense syllables or the words "hallelujah" or "glory, glory, glory." But I rebelled against this method. I didn't want to fake anything. I didn't want the Spirit to come as a result of working myself into a frenzy. I wanted it to be real and natural.

When I was about nineteen, I was preaching at a little country schoolhouse near Dyersburg, Tennessee, where one of my older brothers lived. My brother wasn't able to come to my crusade, but his wife did.

That night, from my room, I could hear their voices. My brother asked her, "How did Lester do?"

Loud and clear, I heard her reply, "Lester won't make it if he preaches a thousand years!"

Stunned, I began to cry before the Lord. I could not understand. I cried out to the Lord and asked Him if it was time to quit preaching. I lay on the floor, hurting all over and asking for an answer.

I got one. "NO!" He said. "You can't quit! Read Luke 4:18!"

Opening my Bible, I read: "The Spirit of the Lord is upon me, because he hath anointed me to preach the gospel to the poor; he hath sent me to heal the broken-hearted, to preach deliverance to the captives and recovering of sight to the blind, to set at liberty them that are bruised, to preach the acceptable year of the Lord."

"Lord, do You mean that?" I asked.

"Yes, I do," He said. "My Spirit is upon you and, when people meet you, they will know you are a person that My Spirit is upon."

"Really?" I said.

"Yes," He said. "You're not always going to be out here in country schoolhouses. You're in training now. My Spirit is upon you, and I have anointed you!"

I studied that verse carefully. I had been taught that I was supposed to manifest Holy Spirit Baptism by sudden and dramatic speaking in tongues.

Yet, nothing happened.

One night, after ten people had been saved and filled with the Holy Spirit in my meeting, I came home dejected. Although I had been down at the altar seeking the Baptism with the rest of them, I hadn't received anything.

I went back to the room and lay on my bed, discouraged. As I stared up at the ceiling, I mumbled aloud to myself, "What's wrong with me?"

God answered: "You have felt that you could just grab anything you wanted when and how you wanted it."

I was so convicted.

It was true: I had decided that people got the Holy Spirit by pushing the right buttons. I felt that if you followed certain formulas, God had to respond.

It doesn't work that way. God cannot be bullied. He does not take orders. You cannot earn the Holy Spirit.

So, He let me go down my check list and find that sometimes, He does nothing — even in response to a sincere, fervent prayer.

Sometimes the answer is, "No."

That's why He had humiliated me in front of scores of churches by giving thousands of my converts the gift of the Holy Spirit — but withholding it from me.

Now that He had my attention, the Lord told me simply: "Since you didn't receive the Holy Ghost your way, I am going to give the Spirit to you as a free gift."

In that moment, God's glory filled the room. The Spirit seemed to flow throughout my whole being, and I began to speak in a heavenly language.

Today as I see such terrible materialism sweeping this nation — and our churches — I know why the Lord was intent on showing me that He does not take orders.

He is God— and we are not.

Over the years, I have seen many disillusioned believers fall away from the Lord because they proclaimed a packaged incantation for Him to cure their loved one or bless them with riches. But God did not respond their way. He does not take orders.

"I received a blessing last night," I announced at breakfast to the folks where I was staying. They glanced around knowingly. "Everybody knows it," said the farm wife with a smile.

Nothing else was said. I don't know whether I disturbed their sleep — or if the presence of the Lord was manifested to each of them or what — but I know that after I received the Holy Spirit, my sermons improved.

I plunged into my calling with renewed joy. Now I had the Spirit of God working within me. It was wonderful.

But another incredible blessing soon awaited me.

8

Where in the World Is Howard Carter?

T he night I received the vision of the millions plunging into hell, four thousand miles away in London, England, a thirty-nine-year-old Bible college president named Howard Carter was praying. God began speaking to him, and the message so moved Brother Carter that he wrote it down: "I have found a companion for thee: I have called a worker to stand beside thee. He hath heard My call, he respondeth and he joineth thee in the work to which I have called thee.

"I have called him, although thou hast not seen him. He is called and chosen and shalt join thee. Behold, he cometh — he cometh from afar. He cometh to help thee to carry thy burden and be a strength at thy side, and thou shalt find pleasure in his service at thy side, and thou shalt delight in his fellowship.

"He shalt come at the time appointed and shalt not tarry. At a time thou thinkest not shalt he appear, even when thou art engaged in My work — and this is what he will say: 'Wherever you go, I will go. Over the highest mountains, over the tempestuous waves of the sea, into the deep valleys, into the plains. I will succor you, I will assist you, I will strengthen you, I will help you, and in every time of need I shall be with you. When you are old, I will strengthen you and assist you and help you. I shall succor you in your old age, and you shall be unto me as a father.' "

Brother Carter pondered over the words. He was the general superintendent of a large British denomination and the president of a prestigious Bible college, but he was almost forty years old and had never been married. So, for a moment, it seemed the Lord was sending him a wife — but this word from God said "*He* shall come from afar."

That meant God wasn't talking about marriage.

Brother Carter read the message to his staff at the Hampstead Bible College. "Oh, you are going to get married," said one professor. "God is going to bring you a pretty woman from some far country."

Carter shook his head. No, he explained, the message clearly said "he" cometh, "he" cometh from afar, "he" cometh to help thee. The prophecy didn't say anything about a woman. God was going to send a man to travel with him.

Brother Carter then read it to the student body. "This is a prophecy," he told them. "If I am a false prophet, mark me as one and discard me — but if this comes true, then you will know that I am a prophet of God."

One of the students said, "Yes, we will. Is it a woman?"

Brother Carter read it back to them and said, "It says 'he.' It cannot be a woman."

Daily, Carter expected the promised helper to arrive. Eighteen months passed, and Carter was thinking that perhaps he should make a trip to the Far East to visit some of his denomination's missionaries in the field.

When he received an unexpected invitation to speak to a camp meeting at Eureka Springs, Arkansas, he immediately declined since the Ozark Mountains of the United States were not even remotely on his way to the Far East. He thanked them for thinking of him but offered his regrets. He forgot about the invitation.

Then, he received a telegram from Arkansas, asking when he would be arriving. Apparently his letter had not arrived.

The wording of the telegram moved him unexpectedly. But the conference was so short. Was it a good use of the Lord's money to travel so far out of his way to such a brief meeting?

He sought the Lord, locking himself in a church sanctuary, asking for a clear word from God. In his solitude, he felt the Lord telling him: "Go thou for the journey and clothe thee for the path which thou shall take, for I am sending thee and I will go with thee. Thou hast waited for Me and thou hast done well, for thy waiting has been thy wisdom, and thou hast shown the path and I will give thee grace to treat it. Thou shalt speak My words and shalt follow My leading and do My will."

The message went on to assure Carter it was God sending him out and it was not any human desire that was urging him to go. The Lord showed him that his task was to go to the nations "where My servants labor. Thou shalt comfort My people and cheer those who have labored for Me. In dark places shalt thou give them help, for I am with thee."

Carter knew he should go to Arkansas. He sent a transatlantic cablegram, "Ignore letter, am accepting."

I often recalled my vision and grew restless as I waited for God to open the door for me to fulfill it. I wanted to minister to the nations so badly that I didn't know what to do.

I had never heard of Howard Carter, and he had never heard of Lester Sumrall, the "Little Preacher."

Meanwhile, I was preaching in Oklahoma — I think it was in the town of Seminole — and staying with a family that lived out in the country. I had gotten up early that morning to go out to the pine trees where I often went to pray. There, the Lord spoke to me and said, "I want you to go to Eureka Springs today."

I said, "What for?"

He said, "They're having a camp meeting over there. I want you to go."

I went in the house and told my sister, "Put all of our stuff in the car. We're going to leave. We'll go by and tell the pastor good-bye."

When I told the pastor we had to leave, he got very angry. "That's the trouble with you young preachers," he lashed out at me. "You don't have any respect for your elders. You don't do what you're told. You promised to be here, and you should stay here."

I said, "I know we are supposed to keep our word. Nevertheless, God, told me to go to this camp meeting. I'm sorry, but this has never happened before. God told me to go, and I've got to go. You can preach the meeting and then dismiss it."

The pastor was furious and said I would never amount to anything and that a man who wouldn't keep his word was worthless.

"Well, talk to God about it," I told him. "I didn't cause it. God told me to go to Eureka Springs, and I have to go."

"I'm going to tell all the pastors never to have you," he roared. "I'll tell them that you are not to be trusted, that you quit in the middle of the week. Furthermore I'm not going to give you any money."

"I don't want any money," I said. "I didn't ask you for any money. I only told you that God told me to go to Eureka Springs, Arkansas to a camp meeting, and I have to go."

"That's not of God. You are wrong."

It was like talking to a brick wall. All he could think of was his personal embarrassment and the inconvenience of having to finish up the crusade himself.

"God bless you," I told him as I left.

I have never seen him since.

My sister Leona and I drove the mountainous 150

miles to Eureka Springs, Arkansas, up in the beautiful
Ozarks that day. Although it wasn't very far, the trip up
into the mountains took most of the morning since the
roads were so twisting and turning.

By the time we arrived, the meetings had already
started.

Two foreigners were the guest speakers — Howard
Carter from England and a man from Germany named
Otto J. Klink. Being a Southerner that didn't set too well
with me. I didn't like trying to listen to people when you
can't quite understand them.

That morning the Englishman, who was the president of Hampstead Bible college in London was speaking.
I didn't know anything about him or his school, and I
could hardly understand a word he said since his British
accent was so thick.

He used odd words. A truck was a "lorrie" and its
engine was under the "bonnet" instead of the hood. An
elevator was "a lift." But, I sat and listened. He was
lecturing on the gifts of the Spirit. I had never heard
anyone teach on the gifts before. I was absolutely amazed.

I didn't know that there were nine gifts of the Spirit.
I would have guessed forty-four.

After Dr. Carter finished teaching, he walked out
onto the sidewalk, and I followed him. Shaking his hand,
I said, "Thank you for the Word of God that you taught
us."

Then I began to say the funniest thing you ever heard.
Out of my mouth came the words, "Wherever you go, I
will go. Over the highest mountains, over the tempestuous waves of the sea, into the deep valleys, into the
plains."

He was very polite and just stood there, shaking his
head back and forth. I started to leave and more words
welled up again inside of me. They didn't come from my
head but from my spirit. "I will succor you, I will assist
you," I told him. "I will strengthen you, I will help you,

and in every time of need I shall be with you. When you are old, I will strengthen you and assist you and help you. I shall succor you in your old age, and you shall be unto me as a father."

I did not understand what this meant. I stopped and apologized to him. "Sir, excuse me, but I've never done this before. If you will just excuse me, I'll just be going. I'm sorry. I don't usually talk like that to people."

He smiled at me and said, "Come with me to my hotel room and I will tell you why you have spoken as you have."

We walked the half block to his hotel and went up to his room where he introduced me to a man named Stanley Frodsham, the editor of a well-known Christian magazine.

While I waited, Howard Carter and Mr. Frodsham went over to the corner of the room and began whispering to one another. They wouldn't let me in on it. Howard Carter was saying this and that and pointing to pages in a little black notebook.

Then they both turned to me and said, "It seems that God has done something very unusual today."

I replied, "Oh? All I know is that I talked funny."

"What are you?" he asked.

"I'm an evangelist."

"Do you have any intention of being a missionary?"

"A missionary? I'm on my way around the world right now!"

"You are? How long ago did you get this calling?"

"Eighteen months, when I had a vision of the world going to hell."

They looked at one another in absolute disbelief.

Then Howard Carter said, "Do you know that God gave me a prophecy eighteen months ago?"

When we compared times, we realized it was the same day that God had given me my vision.

He said, "God told me that he had a traveling companion for me. He would come from afar. You are four thousand miles from London. This is what you were to say." And he showed me the little black book.

"Look at what you said on the sidewalk. That is what the prophecy said. You gave the Word of God exactly as God gave it to me in London."

He asked, "Are you willing to travel with me?"

"I'm willing to travel with anybody. I'm ready to go," I said.

He looked straight at me and said, "You are the one!"

My vision was being realized!

"Do you want to join me?" he asked.

"Well," I answered, "if that's what the Lord wants. He's told me that I have to go."

"All right," he went on. "I'll teach and you be the evangelist, because I am not an evangelist at all. I'll lay hands on people to receive the Holy Ghost, and you lay hands on the people to be healed."

"Oh, that sounds real good to me," I replied. "Thank you, I'll do that."

So we agreed to travel the world and pursue a world-wide missionary venture together. It was glorious!

He said, "I'm going to the West Coast."

I walked out of the hotel and went back down to the car where my sister was waiting. "We're finished here," I said. "We're going home."

My parents had moved to Mobile, Alabama so we headed south down the highway.

"You know," I said, "I met this Mr. Carter."

"Yes, I thought maybe you had. I saw you walking together."

"He wants me to travel with him."

"Is that right?" she asked.

"Yes, but I made one mistake. I forgot to ask him his address and he never asked for mine, so I didn't give it to him. I've already lost him." So I lost him the same hour that I found him.

When we arrived at my parents' home, I prayed

about it, and the Lord said, "Sell your car, get a passport, and go west."

So I obeyed.

It took two or three weeks to get my passport from Washington, DC. I sold my car and got enough money to travel.

Although I had no idea where to find Brother Carter, I headed to California.

I got on a train in Mobile, the *Sunset Limited* and started toward Los Angeles. That was a good name for that train because the sun set a lot of times before I arrived in California.

Crossing Texas was like taking a trip around the world. I woke in Texas and went to bed in Texas. I thought, *Oh, God, when is Texas ever going to end?*

The train stopped at every little town and for about two days, the conductor yelled, "Texas!"

"Ain't there anything else?" I asked sarcastically.

"Not around here there isn't," was his reply.

When we finally arrived in California, I got off the train and waited. I did not see Carter anywhere. I just assumed he would be at the station. For this small-town boy who had just spent several years preaching among farmers and oil field workers, Los Angeles looked mighty big. I had no idea where to look for Carter.

I decided the best thing to do was to find a church. I knew one of the largest churches in Los Angeles was Bethel Temple, so I went there and introduced myself to Dr. Turnbull, the pastor.

"I'm Lester Sumrall," I said.

"Oh," he replied, "I'm glad you made it!"

"Why?" I asked.

"Well, Howard Carter said you would be coming here and told me to take good care of you. We have a hotel room for you, and we want you to preach for us."

"Who was here?" I asked.

"Howard Carter."

"And he said I would be here?"

"Oh, yes. We've been looking for you."

I thought, *Now wait a minute here.* We'd had no communication at all since the day I met him at Eureka Springs. I didn't know where he was, and he couldn't have known where I would be. But he had told people I would be coming. It scared me to realize I was moving into a world that I didn't understand at all.

"Where is he?" I asked hopefully.

"I think he's in Japan," Dr. Turnbull answered.

Japan? He had left without me! I was baffled but not completely discouraged.

Looking back, I realize that this was quite an extraordinary conversation. This well-known pastor of a large church wanted me to preach although he had known me for only fifteen minutes. I was ecstatic. A teen-ager like me being able to walk into the largest church in Los Angeles and have them welcoming me as if I were some kind of celebrity. It was unbelievable.

After I preached there, I went looking around and saw a church near the beach. When I went in and introduced myself, the pastor said, "My, you're welcome. My, we're so glad to see you."

"Why? I haven't written you before," I said, puzzled by his response.

"Well, Howard Carter was here."

"Is that right?" I asked, "What did he say?"

"He told us that you'd be here and that we're to take good care of you."

"Do you know where I can find Howard Carter?" I questioned. "You two are friends, aren't you?"

"Yes, very bosom like," the pastor said in his thick British accent. "We are both Englishmen from London."

"Where is he?"

"In China," he replied.

I said to myself, *Well Japan has a hundred million, and China has five hundred million. Well, I guess I can find him among six hundred million.*

Lillian Yoemans, a godly woman who taught at the nearby L.I.F.E. Bible College, was also a very close friend of Dr. Carter, and he had told her about me.

"Come over for dinner," she told me.

Before we sat down for the meal, she said, "Kneel on that little prayer carpet. God's Holy Ghost is in it."

I was from the hills of Arkansas and the plains of Oklahoma and the tall timber of Mississippi and Alabama and Florida. I was pretty down to earth and not into magic carpets, but I obeyed. After all, she was a medical doctor and eighty-five years old.

When I knelt down, she began to pray for me. I don't know about her carpet, but she had God's power. When we got through, I said, "Do you know where Howard Carter is?"

She said, "Yes, he's in India."

I thought, *Dear God, between a hundred million in one place and a billion in another and another 500 million in another, I'll find him for sure. So, I'll go search for him.*

Something inside of me said, "Why don't you pray about it."

If we would pray rather than talk, we would get along so much better.

So I prayed, "Lord, how am I going to find this man?"

The Lord said, "You didn't ask Me at all about it. You asked other people."

"Oh, dear, I made a mistake there," I confessed. "Where should I go?"

The Lord said, "Go to the bottom of the world and work up." The Lord sometimes has the most unusual ways of telling you what to do. He didn't tell me where Brother Carter was at all. He said, "Go to the bottom."

I asked, "What's the bottom?"

"Australia," He answered.

Fine, but up to that point nobody had said Mr. Carter was in Australia. They said he was in India, China, and Japan.

I said, "Well, I guess that's all right." After all, I had no idea where Brother Carter was.

I had already purchased a ticket to Japan, so I went and changed it — which was a miracle in itself. In those days boat companies weren't always nice about refunding money, especially if you were going to buy a ticket from their competitor — and this was during the Depression. But they didn't give me any trouble.

I purchased another ticket to Australia, but my meager savings were dwindling. I had just enough for a one-way fare, and $12 left over.

One of the ministers, three times my age, drove me to the pier the day I was to set sail. Concerned about my welfare, he inquired into my finances.

Since Howard Carter and I had agreed to travel entirely by faith in the provision of God, I considered it none of his affair.

"But, my dear young man," the brother said, "you will starve."

"Then will you please send a small tombstone," I replied, "and have it inscribed, 'Here lies Lester Sumrall — starved to death trusting Jesus!' "

Those were brave words, but after I boarded the ship and went down to my little room, I began to weep. Here I was heading into the vast unknown. I didn't know what I was doing, where I was going, or how long I would be gone. Already one preacher had said I would starve to death.

After a while, I pulled myself together and decided to evangelize the people on the ship. The response, however, proved less than overwhelming. An infidel verbally tore me to shreds, and some church people made fun of me for being a faith preacher. The devil gave it to me for thirty days. What a trip that was!

After twenty-one days, we arrived in Wellington, New Zealand. I was so sick and tired of that ship that I had to get off.

Tomorrow I'm going into town, I said to myself.

Since the boat mostly carried freight, cargo had to be loaded and unloaded. I knew this would take many hours, so I ate an early breakfast and left the ship. Then I walked all over Wellington trying to find a church that had heard of Howard Carter.

Little did I know that he was also in New Zealand.

On his way to Tokyo, Carter had stopped off in Honolulu, Hawaii and preached at a meeting. While he was there, he received a cable from New Zealand saying, "We are having a ministers' retreat up in the mountains, and our speaker got desperately ill. Would you please come and help us?"

A boat was leaving for Wellington out of Honolulu that day. So rather than going to Tokyo, he changed his ticket and set sail for New Zealand.

On the day my ship pulled into Wellington harbor, Howard Carter was at that minister's retreat up in the mountains.

That afternoon, as he was kneeling by his bed praying, he said, "God you gave me a traveling companion to go with me. Lord, I'm concerned about that young man. You said he would be with me and that he would stay with me. You said he would bless me. I haven't heard a word from him for several months. He's lost."

The Lord replied, "I haven't lost him."

Carter said, "Seems to me like we've both lost him."

"No," the Lord reassured him, "he's on a boat down there in the harbor right now in Wellington. He'll get off tomorrow morning and spend several hours looking for churches in Wellington. He'll be looking for the Assembly of God Church — and he'll find it at eleven o'clock in the morning. Send a note down there and tell him to go on to Australia and that you'll meet him over there when you're through here."

Brother Carter came out of his prayer room and asked the group of preachers, "Which one of you is from Wellington?"

A great big New Zealander stood up and answered, "I am."

"Will you go home?" Brother Carter asked. "I have a young American friend who is arriving and will be at your house tomorrow morning. Give him this card."

On the back of the card, Carter had written, "Go on to Australia, and I will meet you there in three months in Sydney." That's all it said.

"How do you know that he is in Wellington?" they asked.

"The Holy Spirit told me," answered Brother Carter. He knew it through his gift of the word of God's knowledge. God was always giving Brother Carter supernatural knowledge of something that he couldn't see with his eyes or hear with his ears.

These New Zealanders were so stirred up they said, "Well, go on. See if he is a liar or not. See what kind of a teacher we've got. Come back and tell us."

The big New Zealander preacher got in his car and sped down to his home in Wellington. He and his wife waited all day for somebody to come who was an American.

When I got off the boat, I didn't know what kind of church to look for. I thought maybe the city had an Assembly of God, one of the churches my mother had attended when I was little. I walked over to a big church, but it was a Church of England. I asked, "Have you ever heard of the Assemblies of God?"

They said, "No."

I met a man on the street and asked, "Have you ever heard of a church called the Assemblies of God?"

He laughed and said, "Sinners of God. That's a great name. I could join up."

"I didn't say sinners of God. I said Assemblies of God."

"No, I've never heard anything like that," he replied.

I went to the Salvation Army, to the Presbyterians,

and to the Baptists. From eight o'clock in the morning until eleven, I walked all over the city, but nobody had ever heard of the Assemblies of God. I even went to the courthouse.

Leaning against a light post in downtown Wellington, I said, "Lord, I'm sure there is an Assembly of God church in this city. I've heard of Smith Wigglesworth being here, and I've heard of the revivals. I wish I could find it."

A man came walking down the street, and the Lord put something in my heart.

When he got closer, I said, "Hey, come here. I am looking for a church that will meet together sometimes all day and they say 'Hallelujah.'"

He looked at me rather strangely, then responded, "Yeah, yeah! Over across the railroad tracks. You go that way out of town, then go to the left and on a little hill you will find it there."

I followed his directions and soon came to a small church perched on the top of a knoll. It probably wouldn't seat a hundred, but I couldn't help but admire the beauty of the building with its little steeple and white steps leading to a small porch. Beside the church was a parsonage that looked like a doll house.

I went up and knocked on the door.

A great big man opened the door, filling the entire space with his body, and said in a deep, resounding, pastor's voice, "Yes?"

A less timid guy than myself would have run off the porch and back down the hill.

I said, "You don't know me . . ."

"Yes, I do."

"No, you don't know me."

"Yes, I do."

"I've never written to you, and I don't even know your name and you don't know me!"

"You are Lester Sumrall."

I stared at him in disbelief. "My goodness," I said,

"Howard Carter is in this country, isn't he?"

"Yes. Come on in."

"Where is Howard Carter?" I asked.

"Oh, he's a hundred miles, up in the mountains," the pastor replied. "Here's a card from him. He wants you to go on to Australia, and he'll meet you over there."

He handed me the little card.

I thanked him and walked back to the boat to continue my journey to Australia.

It bothered me a little that here I was in New Zealand, just a hundred miles from Howard Carter, and he was sending me away. On the other hand, I didn't want to see him at all. This Howard Carter seemed to be so spiritual that it made me a little uncomfortable. If I had given it much thought, I probably would have decided I didn't want to be around anybody that close to God. How could I ever live up to him?

Obediently, I continued on to Australia.

By this time, I had spent most of my remaining twelve dollars, and the prophecy of the preacher back in California had been ringing in my ears.

Yes, I was about to be stranded — where I would almost certainly starve to death — but that was not what God had in mind.

He watched to see if I would obey.

9

The Tender Englishman

After arriving in Australia, I quickly got acquainted with the local churches and was invited to speak to several congregations.

My first meeting was held in Melbourne. The pastor had a church of about a thousand people and invited me to hold a week-long evangelism crusade. When the week was over, however, he didn't give me any offering. Like many foreigners, he automatically assumed that all Americans were rich.

He told me, "It is very interesting to me to meet a young American who can afford to travel all around the world."

I said, "I may be traveling, but what I didn't tell you was that, when I left America, I only had twelve dollars."

He was astonished. "I'm surprised that Australian immigration even let you into the country!" he said. Usually, if you don't have a ticket to get home, they won't even let you get off the ship.

"How are you going to survive?" he asked.

"Faith!" I responded simply.

I had no pledges of support. I didn't even tell the state

conference of the denomination that had licensed and ordained me that I was leaving the country. I certainly didn't ask them for any support. No churches were backing me, and nobody in my family was sending me money.

Now here I was in Australia, and the first place I preached didn't give me any money.

That Sunday night at the end of the week of meetings, I returned to the home where I had been staying. "Lord," I prayed, "I don't have any way to leave town."

My next meeting was a couple of hundred miles away, and I had no way to get there. No way at all.

I said to God, "Lord, I've got news for You. I'm not leaving this room until I get a ticket. I'm not going out on the sidewalk with a big suitcase and no ticket. I'm not going to go to the train station and stand there like a fool waiting for a ticket. You have to bring the ticket to this room, or I will die in this room!"

Then my spirit broke, and I laid down on the floor and cried all night because I had no way to get out of town. I was twelve thousand miles away from home, alone, and penniless.

The next morning, the Australians with whom I was staying fixed what smelled like a delicious breakfast. The wife knocked on the door and said, "Brother Sumrall, breakfast is ready."

I said, "I'm not eating. Thank you very much. Go ahead without me."

Remaining alone in my room, I packed my suitcase and put it by the door along with my briefcase and my Bible. I was ready to go, except that I had no ticket.

The family had breakfast around seven o'clock, and then the husband went to work. The wife busied herself around the house.

At eight o'clock she came back to the door, knocked on it, and said, "Brother Sumrall, are you there?"

I answered, "Yes, I'm here."

"There's a man here to see you from the church. Will you see him?"

"Yes!"

I excitedly opened the door to see a big, fine looking Australian man standing before me. He was crying.

I said to myself, *Oh no, another pitiful tale,* assuming the man needed some kind of personal counseling. It was not unusual for people to seek out a visiting preacher instead of confiding in their local pastor.

I was twenty years old now, but I knew enough to know I was not called to be a counselor. *That's someone else's mission,* I told myself. *I'm an evangelist.*

The man said, "I couldn't sleep last night."

"I couldn't sleep either, so what of it?"

"If this isn't right, I will never try it again."

"What are you talking about?" I asked.

He said, "I have no idea. We know that you are rich."

I smiled.

He said, "You are to preach in . . . ." and he named the town. I agreed.

"Tonight," he said, looking at me.

Again I agreed.

"Do you realize that the train that goes over there is a Special, and that nobody rides it without a special reservation? Do you have a reservation?"

I said, "Sir, I didn't even know that it was a reserved train."

He said, "God told me you were not acquainted with our rail system. God also told me to go and get that reservation for you — and that I should be the one honored to purchase the ticket for you. I know that you don't need it, that you have plenty of money."

He asked, "You don't have a reservation?"

I said, "No."

"Do you have a ticket?"

"No."

"Here they are," he said, holding two tickets in his hand. One was a reservation for the reserved train, and the other one was a ticket to the city. He said, "Let's go."

I put the tickets in my pocket, he took the suitcase, I took my Bible and briefcase, and away we went.

On the way, I told him, "Sir, I received no money for preaching in your church for the week. I had no money to buy that ticket. It was God who told you what to do."

You talk about an Australian being a happy man. That man almost danced in the street to think that God would speak to him at night and tell him about an American that he hardly knew. He had only seen me up in the pulpit and had never even shaken my hand.

All the way to the station we laughed at ourselves and what it takes to trust Almighty God. We also marveled at Him who is able to do all things, abundantly more than we are able to conceive or even think.

"Good-bye,"' I told him as we parted. "I'll meet you in heaven."

God is real. I have known Him to be real.

I held a few more meetings in that area, then went to Brisbane, rented a tent, and had a crusade that lasted several months. A new church was started as a result. Today that church has about a thousand members and is one of the finest churches in Queensland, Australia.

Being an American in Australia worked for me — in that I attracted large crowds — and against me because they couldn't understand my Southern drawl and I couldn't understand their Aussie slang.

One woman declared that it took her a week before she figured out what I was preaching. She said, "I was determined to know what you were talking about. I came every night until I could understand you."

The crusade tent was set up right across the street from a pub. A pub is an Australian tavern.

One night, two drunks began insulting me as I stood in the pulpit ready to preach to about two hundred people. I called two of my ushers up front.

"Will you throw the drunks out, please?" I asked.

"Why?" the ushers asked. "They're not hurting you."

I said, "They are disturbing this meeting."

"Just you," they argued. "They're not disturbing the rest of us."

I tried to preach, but those drunks laughed at me for being an American. They were calling me all sorts of names. Finally I said, "Let's sing a chorus."

While the crowd sang, I walked to the back of the tent and grabbed one of those drunks by his collar, turned him around and kicked him in the seat of his pants. I whacked him once and whacked him again, then I led him toward the door of the tent. When I whacked him one more time, his feet went out from under him.

The other drunk helped him up, and as they were running out the door, they said, "You had better leave that American alone."

When I came back inside, I didn't know if the audience would want to hear what I had to say or not. But to my amazement, the entire group stood to their feet and clapped for five minutes.

The next night we had twice as many people as the first night. Those Australians respected me from then on, and I preached in Brisbane for six weeks.

Then I returned to Sydney to spend Christmas with a congregation who had invited me to hold meetings there.

I had to adjust to being in the Southern Hemisphere and celebrating Christmas in the summertime. It's always a little startling to hear Christmas carols on loudspeakers when it's 90 degrees out and families are talking about spending the holidays at the beach.

During that week of meetings, there were great outpourings of God's blessing that climaxed with a watchnight service on New Year's Eve.

When I heard there was a ship scheduled to dock on New Year's Day, I decided to go down to the wharf. Three months had passed since I had received Howard Carter's card, and I had hoped he might be coming in on this ship.

When I did not see him disembark with the other passengers, I turned away with a heavy heart.

For some reason, however, I stopped at the customs shed — I guess just to make sure.

I have described the scene many times, but here's how I told it in one of the first books I ever wrote, *Adventuring With Christ*, published in 1938.

> On the first day of the year, at 10:30 a.m., I watched the beautiful white S.S. Maraposa as she gracefully steamed into the harbor and docked at her wharf.
>
> With longing eyes, I scanned her crowded deck, but all in vain. Then, in the customs shed, I accidentally came face to face with Brother Carter. Giving bent to my emotions, I heartily embraced him before all. It had now been five months since the Lord had so miraculously brought us together in His Providence and for His work.

You would think that my finding Brother Carter at last would have been incredibly dramatic — like Stanley finding Dr. Livingston in the African jungle. But when I found him that day, he was not particularly surprised nor emotional about it. He endured my hug, but I can't even remember exactly what we said.

He didn't cry or shout hallelujahs. He just shook my hand.

"I'm glad to be with you," I said excitedly. "We're going to have a good time together."

Of course, he was an Englishman, and they're not very expressive — certainly not in public.

We stayed in the pastor's home there in Sydney where I had been preaching. After Brother Carter came, he preached for two or three days and I sat in on his meetings.

From there we traveled north, then we were separated. That became a pattern of sorts. Because Brother Carter had more invitations to speak than he was able to accept, he would ask if instead they would like to have a young American evangelist who was traveling with him.

The first time we split up, he went down to Melbourne and spoke at a meeting, and I went somewhere else and held a crusade — but we were together much of the time.

Despite his lack of emotional demonstration, he took a liking to me, treating me as if I were his son — although he was just into his forties and I had turned twenty. For a starched, formal Englishman, he could be tender.

If I misspelled a word or used poor grammar, he just showed me how I needed to correct it. He was very well-educated, and I got to the point where I wouldn't send out a letter until he read it.

One day he suggested, "You should write the story of our being together." So I began keeping notes about our experiences, and later wrote the book, *Adventuring With Christ.*

Brother Carter asked me to write for a magazine called *Redemption Tidings* that went all over America, England, and Canada. During the time we were together, I had an article published almost every month in that magazine. The Lord used that magazine to open all sorts of doors.

Years later, when I got to meet that great pioneer of faith, Smith Wigglesworth, he said he had been looking forward to meeting me. *Why?* I wondered. He said he had read about me in the *Redemption Tidings,* and he had always wanted to meet me.

One day as we were sailing from Singapore to Hong Kong, I was standing up by the edge of the boat railing, writing and looking at the sea. Suddenly, my fountain pen just slipped through my fingers and into the ocean. What a loss. In those days a person only had one pen. Nobody had two, and there was no such thing as a cheap ballpoint.

When Brother Carter saw that I wasn't writing any longer, I said, "Oh, my pen's in the South China Sea, I put it to bed. It will never wake up."

He laughed a little bit and said, "Well, that's too bad."

After we arrived in Hong Kong, I went up to our room and found a brand new pen laying on the bed.

"Well, look at that!" I exclaimed.

"Yes, the Lord sent you that," Brother Carter said.

"You're not calling yourself 'Lord,' are you?" I smiled.

He laughed and replied, "Well, you're writing for me really." That was all he said about it.

Brother Carter was just opposite of my father. He was firm but tender and caring. He could show warmth, and he did — but in a very British way. If I needed a shirt, he would get it before I even realized I needed one.

Because of my brash way of talking, people — especially those not used to dealing with Americans — sometimes misunderstood my intentions. But Brother Carter never did.

If I wasn't with him and somebody said something against me, he would say, "That's not true. I've lived with him. You misunderstood him. I can tell you the facts about him."

One time Brother Carter had to defend not only me but himself.

A missionary woman whom we met in Japan had a daughter about eighteen or nineteen years old. When I came along, she thought I would be just the perfect husband for her daughter.

Although I knew the Lord had the right one for me and that I would find her in His perfect timing, I was too serious about my work to think about girls then. After all, my mentor was a bachelor in his forties — expecting to get married someday, but not soon.

In fact, Brother Carter didn't marry for another quarter of a century, when he was in his early sixties. He actually met his future bride at my house, and I was later the best man at his wedding. Before he died, they spent almost three decades together.

While we were having dinner with the missionaries in Japan, this woman spoke up and said, "Brother Carter, why don't you try to be a gentleman like Brother Sumrall is?"

I could have gone through the floor. He was *the* perfect British gentleman, and I was a country bumpkin. Everybody knew that, including me.

Before I could come to his defense, Carter replied, "That is so gracious of you. You know, Brother Sumrall has been working on me for about two years now. You can't imagine the improvement I've made. Thank you."

I thought, *How can a man be that nice?* He knew I was nothing. It didn't take anybody long to find out how roughshod I was.

Embarrassed, I got up from the table and went back to my room. In a little while he came in and, putting both hands on his knees, rocked back and forth with laughter. "Wasn't that the funniest thing you ever heard in your life?"

I said, "No. That was the craziest thing I ever heard in my life. Do you know what she —"

"Oh, sure," he said. "She wants you to marry her daughter."

"Well, I'm not even going to speak to the girl. Let's get out of town."

He just continued to laugh in the way he always did — with both hands on his knees.

We were quite a team — stuffy, British college president full of wisdom and thunder, and his joke-telling, brash, wet-behind-the-ears American confederate. We shared laughter and joy.

Howard Carter was the only man who had ever truly esteemed me.

I could preach the poorest sermon, and he would say, "You know, Mr. Sumrall" — he always called me Mr. Sumrall — "that's a very fine sermon." Then, in his gentle way, he would say, "I can give you a few pointers so that the next time you give it, it will be better."

A master of the English language, he came from a very wealthy background. His father was a successful inventor.

Brother Carter tutored me in public speaking, diction, human relations, and — of course, the Bible. I had the finest instruction on the face of the earth from one of the wisest academics I have ever met.

Although a theologian and scholar, he entered into Bible study with prayer and a desire to be led of the Holy Spirit. I respected him for his sincerity and the fact that he lived by faith but didn't talk about it. His needs were always kept between himself and God.

Always before I had distrusted preachers and disdained the idea of attending any Bible college. I was an "independent," I told myself; the Lord would teach me anything I needed to know.

So, the Lord sent me my own personal Bible college president to be a mentor, big brother, and tutor.

It was on our journey from Australia to the Dutch colony of Java that Brother Carter and I first really became acquainted. We were together for about two weeks on that boat.

I began to love this godly, big-brotherly Englishman, and he began to love this young American kid. He loved me because I was a boy who could laugh.

I was an inspiration to him, and he was certainly an encouragement to me.

Until the day he died, he considered me his Timothy and, in his mind, he had brought me up in the ways of the Lord.

But I knew I had done something for him, too. He was a middle-aged, bachelor preacher who needed a traveling companion — an eager-to-learn Timothy to whom he could be Bible teacher, social tutor, big brother, and spiritual father.

10

Demons At My Coattails

When Brother Carter and I left Australia, we took a ship that had been built as a yacht for the deposed German king, Kaiser Wilhelm. It was gorgeous and too beautiful to be running freight and passengers between Australia and the Dutch East Indies. I'd never seen anything so magnificent in all my life.

The British had confiscated the yacht as a war reparation after they won World War I.

These were the mid-1930s. Hitler had just risen to power in Germany and was moving politically against Austria and Czechoslovakia, but he hadn't launched his *blitzkrieg* against Poland that began World War II or formed his infamous Axis with Italy's Mussolini or Imperial Japan's Tojo.

But the storm clouds of war were gathering.

Mussolini had invaded Ethiopia, and the world had turned a deaf ear to the pleas for help from Emperor Haile Selassie I.

Stalin was tightening his grip on Russia, murdering millions of his own people as he confiscated all private property and forced communism upon the Russian territories that today are independent Kazakstan, Georgia, Belorus, and Ukraine.

Japan had occupied Korea and the Chinese province of Manchuria and was looking lustfully at the Dutch and French colonies that today are Indonesia, Malaysia, Vietnam, and Singapore. Europe, however, was largely at peace, and America was determined to keep out of the trouble being stirred up by Russia, Italy, Germany, and Japan.

The British and Dutch still had vast colonial empires in India, Pakistan, and the East Indies.

We spent three months in densely populated Java, one of the larger, heavily jungled islands of the Dutch East Indies colony off the coast of China — what is now Malaysia, Brunei, and Indonesia.

The people were mostly pagans. Christians were outnumbered by Moslems as well as Chinese and East Indian immigrants who believed in a strange mix of Taoism, Buddhism, Hinduism, and other heathen religions such as demonic spiritualism and ancestor worship.

Astrologers and mediums who could summon "ghosts" of the dead were respected. They made good livings supposedly protecting people from the evil eye and the many devils that they worshipped and feared. Some of the people knew the names of thousands of devil-gods that they said ruled the place. Animal offerings combined with violent self-mutilation and lewd ceremonies were supposed to placate the demons.

The Christians we met talked freely about demon possession and exorcism. When native preachers shared stories about casting out evil spirits, just like Jesus had done in the Bible, I listened very skeptically.

Brother Carter was teaching me how to be a dignified, respectable evangelist, not a holiness devil-chaser like some who advertised in handbills that the public could come see demons cast out or the devil chased out of town. I didn't want to get caught up in that sort of gimmickry. I was no weird mystic, and casting out demons was not for me. I wanted to be rational and sophisticated, like my mentor, Brother Carter.

But God had other ideas.

In Java we had so many invitations, that almost every night Brother Carter would speak in one place and I would speak in another. We would sleep, eat, and study together, so we had daily contact, but our preaching would be in two different places in order to cover more territory.

On one of those speaking engagements in Surabaya, Java, I encountered demon possession for the first time. While I was preaching to a large congregation, maybe fifteen hundred people, I noticed something moving near the front pew. To my horror, a girl of about twelve or thirteen was writhing like a snake on the floor.

She flicked her tongue in and out, and her eyes flashed crazy and wild. It was frightening. She would weave up and down like a cobra. I had never seen anything like it. A repulsive, green foam oozed from her mouth.

No one else seemed to notice or pay her any attention but me. The people just kept singing. Even the men on the platform with me continued to lead the song service, lift up prayers, and read the Bible as if nothing strange was going on.

When are they going to stop that girl? I wondered to myself. *Why don't they do something?*

In the middle of a gospel revival service, this little girl was doing what looked like a pagan snake act or an imitation of a comic-book serpent-woman.

I began to pray, "Lord, help me to save souls despite this thing. I've got to save souls, save souls."

The Lord said, "I'll take care of saving souls, you take care of that problem down there."

Then she began to slither back and forth across the altar area of the church. She would stick out her tongue, move her eyes like a serpent, and foam at the mouth.

I prayed, "Lord, You take care of it."

"No!" God said. "That is *your* problem."

My problem? I thought. *That's new. I've never seen anything like this.*

For at least fifty minutes, she slithered back and forth in front of the altar grinning, always looking at the platform. When she crawled one way, her head turned to face the platform. Then when she crawled back, she looked around to keep facing the platform.

I had no idea what to do nor how to do it. For the whole fifty minutes, I just sat there wishing somebody would take care of the situation, but nobody did a thing about it.

Feelings of hurt and confusion began to overwhelm me. I was a foreigner there, and this was the first time I had ever been in that church. I didn't speak the language.

When the song service ended, I was introduced and stepped up to the pulpit to speak — but I couldn't.

I didn't know what to do. I had never heard a single sermon on demon possession or read a book on exorcism. I knew nothing about deliverance — but I knew that the girl wasn't just being dramatic. She was demon-possessed.

Suddenly, I was stirred with compassion for this little girl who was leering up at me from the aisle. With my interpreter beside me at the pulpit, rather than greeting the people by saying, "Good evening friends. I'm glad to be in Java. It is a beautiful island," or something pleasant like that, I leaned over and pointed toward the little girl and said, "You get up from there and sit in a seat right now!"

I hadn't planned to say that. The words just came out of my mouth.

The interpreter was so startled that he didn't translate a word. Although the girl didn't understand any English and I didn't understand any Javanese, the devil understood.

Immediately, the girl took her hand and wiped the green ooze off of her face, then backed up to the first pew and sat down like a zombie. She didn't move a muscle. During the forty-five minutes that I preached she sat there like a statue.

When I finished my sermon, I leaned back over the pulpit again. This time I shouted, "Now come out of her!"

I'd never heard anyone do that before, but I spoke so loudly they could have heard me down the street.

I did not get close to the girl, but when I spoke, immediately the Spirit of the Lord came upon her. Her eyes came back into focus, and her face that had been contorted changed. Her body relaxed. There was no struggle.

As she came out of that stupor, her eyes became clear. She now had pretty little girl eyes. She looked so sweet.

I knew she had been instantly delivered.

The child looked around her in bewilderment. "Where am I?" she asked. "What am I doing here?" She had been so full of Satan that she didn't even know where she was or how she had gotten there.

The pastor told her that she had been freed from an evil spirit.

She shouted her delight and told us how she'd been oppressed by this demon for quite some time but did not know how to get free from it.

"Is the demon gone now?" I asked her.

"Yes, yes!" she shouted joyfully. By the power of the Holy Spirit, she was set free.

Suddenly, hundreds of people came running down the aisles to be set free, to be delivered, to be saved. I didn't have to ask them to come. When they saw that she was set free, they rushed forward!

When we finally closed the meeting, I went back to my room feeling terribly depressed. It had been a nasty experience. I regretted what I had done.

"I got into a mess tonight," I confessed to Brother

Carter as I told him the details.

He laughed. "You did exactly the right thing."

"But," I protested, "my reputation is shot."

"Forget it," advised the famous preacher.

"Brother Carter, you may not want to travel with me anymore."

"Why is that?" he asked.

"It was pretty nasty. I screamed, and I don't know why I screamed. The girl was set free and a few hundred people got saved."

"W . . . E . . . L . . . L . . ." — you've got to know Englishmen to appreciate how he said it — "it sounds all right to me."

"Does it really?" I asked.

"Yes."

"I hope it never happens again," I said. "I hope I'm finished with that sort of thing."

"W . . . E . . . L . . . L, we'll see," he said.

"I screamed at her," I told him. "She got set free, but I have never done anything like that in church before."

Brother Carter just smiled and remarked, "It sounds all right to me."

It may have sounded all right to him, but I was not sure it was all right with me. I had never seen such a thing in my life!

"I don't know," I told him. "I think my reputation is shot."

He just smiled knowingly. "Forget it," he advised.

I tried. "Lord," I prayed fervently, "I don't want to be a demon chaser."

Because of that experience, I was hesitant to go out on my own again for a while. Seeing how shaken and worried I was about my reputation, Brother Carter agreed that perhaps we should stay together if possible.

In those countries, however, we had so many people begging for us to come that eventually we had to go our separate ways again — he to teach pastors, I to evangelize the lost.

A week later, I found myself in another city where once again the church was packed with hundreds of people. They had even put chairs down the middle of the aisles.

As I walked in with my interpreter, I had to ease my way through the crowd. The aisle was narrow because of the chairs and about a third of the way down, a woman caught me by my coat and wouldn't let go.

She smiled warmly and began caressing my hand in a very erotic manner. Her intentions were clearly seductive. I was so shocked I wanted to slap her.

Instead, I thought, *This is a primitive part of the world. It wouldn't look right for the preacher to just start hitting people.*

But she wouldn't let go of my coat.

The interpreter walked right on in and got up on the platform. How could I take the pulpit when somebody was holding onto my coat?

I could have done like Joseph in the Book of Genesis when he had to get away from Potiphar's lustful wife. I could have left my coat in her hands, but I needed it and didn't want to give it to her.

Finally, I dropped my briefcase and she grinned a strange smile while her eyes darted like serpent fangs. She said in English, "You have a black angel in you and I have a white angel in me," and ended her sentence with a hideous giggle.

The Spirit of the Lord rose up within me. I became angry.

I brought up the arm that she was holding. I took the other hand and gripped both sides of her head and proclaimed, "You are a liar! I have Jesus in me! He is clean! He is pure! You have the devil in you with the blackness of hell. Demon, come out of her!" You could hear me all over that church and out in the yard.

I hadn't been taught to do things like that.

Instantly, she released my coat. Her contorted face changed. She smiled and her eyes softened. Joy filled her and she released me. The craziness was out of her eyes.

I asked her, "How long have you been like that?"

She replied, "Fifteen years ago, I went to a witch doctor with some domestic troubles. That is when the spirit possessed me. I have been abnormal ever since. But when you commanded that evil spirit to come out, it left me. It is gone now."

But I could tell she was not completely freed. "Come out of there, every demon that is within her, and be free!" I proclaimed, and free she became.

We had a great church service that night. The glory of God fell on the entire audience.

I didn't have to preach long. I just exhorted the people for a few minutes, and the crowds came rushing down to give their hearts to God.

As I prayed for them at the altar, I began to put things together. If you set people free from the devil's power, all kinds of people get saved.

The Lord whispered to me, "If you can bind the strong man, you can spoil his house."

I realized that all sinners are the devil's prey. When you bind him first, even before you preach, then you can get the prey. You can get the ones he has been holding captive in his prison house. You jar his gates loose when you first set the people free.

I went back to my room and said, "Brother Carter, wait 'til you hear what happened today. I'm sure you won't ever want to travel with me again. The last time I didn't even get close to the girl, but this time I just grabbed that woman —"

"That sounds all right to me," he said.

"But it's not in the Bible," I said, "I don't want to be doing what's wrong."

"Anytime people are set free, that's good."

"Well, I just wish it wouldn't happen anymore. I

want to be a preacher like you — with dignity and brilliance."

"You will be," he said. "That's all right. This other is very necessary. When it happens, let it go."

We traveled throughout the whole island of Java where, at that time, over fifty million people lived. In almost every city, God provided a deliverance that everyone in the service could witness. Time after time the hearts of the people were opened to the saving message of the gospel by the display of the power of God over evil.

I soon learned that I was not personally in the conflict. It was Christ in me. Also, it was not the person who caused the battle, but the devil within him or her.

I discovered there was no reason to fear. Although the demon-possessed would scream and tear themselves, they did not seek to harm or touch me. I was perfectly safe in exorcising demons.

In fact, the demons usually wanted to run away and avoid confronting me. Through their captives, they would often say, "We are not here. We are gone. Leave us alone."

Almost every time these incidents took place, I would be ministering alone. Brother Carter wouldn't be there with me. At first, I thought the devil was manipulating situations to try to pick on me because I was young and new in the Lord's work. Then I realized God was using each experience to train me, and He had even provided me with my own trustworthy teacher.

Brother Carter had already preached around the world and had encountered every possible situation that a traveling missionary can face. As we discussed each incident, he would assure me and teach me from God's Word how to deliver people from the power of the devil.

When we ministered together, we had tremendous revivals.

Thousands of people received the in-filling of the Holy Spirit when Mr. Carter laid his hands on them. I would minister to them, and many would be instantly healed by God's power and give their hearts to Jesus. We made a remarkable team.

We were like Paul and Timothy together — an older one and a younger one, moving in strength and vigor throughout the world.

11
Bandits and Healing in Tibet

B rother Carter and I next traveled into war-torn mainland China, where the Imperial Japanese were fighting Chinese President Chiang Kai-shek in the east. The Communists, led by the Marxist atheist Mao Tse-tung, were undermining Chiang's ability to govern in the north and, aided by Russian armor, were massacring whole villages.

Many missionaries were executed throughout China as war raged on many fronts. Local chieftains and loyal-ists to the deposed emperor vied for power with the Communists, the Republican Army, the Japanese, and the Russians, fighting and destroying the beautiful, legend-ary land that is China. Chiang Kai-shek, the head of the Republican government of China, was doing the best he could.

On mule back we journeyed into Tibet. This tiny nation high in the Himalayan Mountains on the border with India and Nepal was supposed to be free of conflict — at least that's what we'd been told. But we soon discovered that all respect for the law had disintegrated.

Bloodthirsty bandits and rival warlords terrorized

the countryside. We saw highland villages completely destroyed and ancient Buddhist lamaseries burned, their thousand-year-old books ripped apart and fluttering in the wind. Pools of blood formed grisly lakes where massacres had killed entire hamlets.

Our first scrape with death came when we were crossing the mountains in a mule caravan. We had been ascending for hours when our guide warned us to stay together and keep moving since this area was full of robbers.

As we were nearing the pass, Brother Carter and I dismounted to drink from a spring, then walked on, chatting together, easily keeping up with the slow-moving mules. When we turned a sharp curve around a huge boulder, three men stepped out from the high grass and trees, leveling guns on us.

"Brother Carter," I gasped. "Bandits." I could see the cold bloodlust in their eyes.

"No doubt," he whispered in his wry, British way.

Ragged and filthy, they aimed their guns at us and ordered us to do something I did not understand.

I leaned over to our interpreter and asked, "What did they say?"

With his face full of terror, he whispered, "Get off that mule." Carefully, he slid off of his mule.

Brother Carter and I just stood there. We didn't put up our hands or anything. Then in their language, the armed men ordered us to "March!"

Brother Carter and I got out in front of my mule. Our interpreter walked along there beside us.

The mules in our caravan carried food and supplies and several boxes of local currency. We really weren't carrying much money, but due to their terrible wartime inflation, one of our dollars equaled twenty-five hundred of their almost worthless currency units. To buy food, a person needed almost a wheelbarrow of cash.

One of the bandits stepped up and leveled his rifle at

the back of my head. I tried not to notice. We obediently marched, like they had said.

As we marched along in silence, the devil began to fill me with fear, saying, "You're going to die. They're going to kill you."

I glanced back at the gun barrel behind my head. "No, I'm not going to die," I answered silently. "I didn't come up here to die."

After about three hours, however, I couldn't stand it any longer and said, "God, did I come to Tibet to die?"

He said, "No."

So, I told Him, "Then tell that to this bandit leader back there. He needs to know it, too."

The Lord said, "Your answer is in Revelation 19:6." So I carefully slipped my hand up to my vest and took out the little Testament that I carried in my pocket. As Brother Carter glanced at me quizzically, I began to read it. I was simply amazed: "And I heard as it were the voice of a great multitude."

The devil said, "See? You're going to be in heaven in a few minutes. You're hearing the voice of a great multitude."

I said, "No, that's not it." I kept reading: "And then I heard the voice of many waters."

I said silently, "Yeah, that's it. On Jordan's stormy banks I stand and cast a wistful eye."

We were by those waters, all right. I kept reading. "Then I heard the voice of mighty thunderings saying hallelujah. The Lord God omnipotent reigneth."

That line came alive. I began to laugh. I turned around and laughed in the bandit's face.

He was so startled that the gun barrel pointed at my head dipped to the ground. He just stared at me. Through my interpreter I screamed at him, "What do you want anyway?"

"Well, we don't have any money," said the shaken bandit — through our interpreter. "We need money."

Remember, one of our dollars was twenty-five hundred of theirs.

So I said, "Get him a box."

We gave them a box.

He looked and it was real money. You could see from the grin on his face that he was really pleased. Then I said, "What else do you need?"

He told our interpreter, "We don't have any food."

We carried our food in boxes, too. So we gave them a box of food — rice and beans and so forth.

I asked him, "Now, what do you want?"

He didn't know what to say.

So, I just got on my mule and rode away, followed by the rest of our group. The bandits stared after us in disbelief, then went into the forest and were gone.

We rode on around the side of a mountain on the path that came down into a village. The people ran out to greet us, shouting, "You're alive!"

We said, "Yes, we're alive. What do you mean?"

"You're the only ones," they told us. "Everybody else got killed today on that road. They met robbers and they're dead."

I had to say "Hallelujah!" If the Lord wants you to live, you'll live. He wanted us to live to proclaim His Word, and we were not harmed.

That was not my closest brush with death, however.

My next encounter came up in the war-torn mountains of southwest Asia.

Like a moving city, we were traveling in a caravan of seventeen mules carrying our food, workers, guides, the cook, and the interpreter. The local water was unfit for us to drink, so we had to boil our own.

Either we didn't boil it long enough to kill the germs, or else perhaps I got too thirsty and took a drink out of one of the porters' canteens — but in any case I became very sick.

Suffering from dysentery, I had a raging fever and

constant diarrhea that sent me running for the bushes about every ten minutes. I couldn't eat anything. We were in the middle of nowhere. There weren't any cities nearby.

I began to hemorrhage and, for about 48 hours, bled from my intestines. The high fever and pain were more terrible than I can describe.

My companions could see something was wrong, but I didn't sit around growling, telling people how sick I was. I hadn't complained, because I had learned that to be a good traveler you have to keep your mouth shut or nobody wants you around.

Usually when we started off in the morning, I would put my mule out in front. But rather than going first that morning, I went last. I don't even know where Brother Carter was in the caravan. With all the usual confusion with the animals kicking and snorting and the Chinese muleteers hitting them on the head with sticks, nobody even noticed me or my condition — but I was last coming out. We left about 7 a.m. from the town and were heading up the trail to go to another city when I got dizzy and I fell off of the mule. I had enough of my wits about me to put the mule's reins — actually, a little rope — around a bush.

Then I lost consciousness. When I fell, nobody saw me. Instead, they all went on ahead, not knowing my desperate situation, and didn't come back to find me until late that night.

I lay unconscious until noon.

When I finally came to on that rocky hillside, I realized I had been healed by God's mighty power. The pain was gone, the fever had left, and the diarrhea had stopped. I was beside myself with excitement and praise.

Although I had not even prayed and asked the Lord for help, He had extended His mercy toward me. It wasn't until some years later when I got back to America that I discovered the reason.

While I was preaching in Mobile, Alabama, a man and his wife who were high school teachers, asked the pastor, "Can Sumrall stay with us tonight?"

He said, "Why, I guess so."

As we sat in their living room enjoying a warm fire and refreshments, they said they had kept all the articles I had written about Brother Carter's and my journeys in *Redemption Tidings.*

Suddenly the wife said, "Do you keep a diary?"

I said, "Yes, I've got a five-year diary."

She said, "Would you read me a day from it?"

"What day? Don't know whether I would or not."

She gave me the date, and I went into my bedroom and opened my diary. The entry was for the day I had gotten healed there on the hillside.

I said, "Oh, I'll read you that one, all right. I was dying of dysentery up there, and the Lord healed me suddenly."

They both began to weep.

I said, "You don't need to cry. I didn't die."

"Well, you haven't heard our story," they replied. "When it was morning over there, it was night here. God spoke to us and told us you were dying but didn't tell us where you were, just said you were dying. We cried out to God, 'Save him, save him. Don't let him die. Save him, save him.' At 11 o'clock, God spoke and said, 'He lives.' "

In comparing our two diaries, I saw, indeed, the same morning that I went unconscious on that mountain hillside, these high school teachers had felt that sharp urgency to pray for me.

They saved my life through their intercession.

As I looked back and forth between our two journals, written 12,000 miles apart, the reality of God hit me.

Intercession *can* save a person's life. I was healed by the prayers of two high school teachers who prayed until they broke through.

That was only one of many times when God's people must have prayed and interceded for me.

In mainland China, Brother Carter and I had to pray for many oppressed people who were taken over by the devil. The same was true in Japan, where little images of devils were everywhere, supposedly to frighten away evil. The people lived in absolute terror. Constantly, we encountered people who were possessed by demons.

When we boarded the Trans-Siberian Express, which was to take us across Stalin's Russia into Europe, I told Brother Carter, "Well, thank God, that's over. We're finally getting away from that Oriental disease. Those people are full of demons. It takes a lot of strength out of me when I have to pray for them. I'm just glad to get out of there."

I actually thought that demon possession occurred only in the Orient and that I'd never encounter it again.

It took nine days to travel from Imperial Japanese-occupied Manchuria across into Poland, which had not yet been invaded by the Nazis. We spent a couple of days in Moscow looking over the city and visiting places like Red Square, one of the few things they showed to tourists.

Then we went on into Poland. We hadn't been there a week when in one of my services, a woman on the front row in a very large meeting, began to say, "Hallelujah, hallelujah!"

I said, "Now that doesn't sound right to me." She always said it at the wrong time, out of step with everybody else. "I wish somebody would stop that woman."

But they didn't.

During the forty-five minutes of preliminaries — the special songs, prayers, congregational singing, reading the Bible — she would shout, "Hallelujah!" It was awful.

I thought, *That's not God, for sure. That's not God.* I didn't know what to do about it. I prayed, "Lord, save souls here tonight. Save souls."

The Lord said, "You have to take care of that problem down there first."

"That's Your problem, Lord."

"That's not My problem," He quickly pointed out.

"That's *your* problem."

Something about that conversation was very famil-iar. It was exactly what I had said to the Lord in Java, when that little girl was writhing like a snake.

Sitting on that platform, I didn't know what I was going to do. I knew I couldn't preach with that woman screeching out, "Hallelujah," and sounding like the devil.

When I walked to the pulpit, rather than greeting the people and saying, "I'm thankful and happy to be with you; God will bless you; it's nice to be in Poland," rather than doing that, I did exactly as I had done in Java.

I leaned over the pulpit and said, "And you shut up!"

That's how I started out my sermon, but rather than shutting up, the woman began to bark like a dog. Ev-erybody in the whole place heard her.

Finally, the ushers were ready to help, but I said to them, "You just sit down. You didn't help when she was screeching out, 'Hallelujah.' So, now, leave her alone."

I leaned on the pulpit and said, "You shut up and come OUT of her!"

Suddenly, she stopped and looked around at the people and smiled.

The Spirit of God fell on that audience and we had a magnificent time. Many people found the Lord Jesus Christ as Saviour. But I was troubled.

In Poland, Germany, France, Holland, Norway, Swe-den, and Denmark, I found cases of demon possession similar to the ones I'd seen in Java, Singapore, Hong Kong, Tibet, Manchuria, Japan, and Korea.

"Hey," I said to Brother Carter, "that Oriental disease has come over here to Europe, hasn't it?"

He just smiled.

12

Confronting the Powers of Darkness

In Nazi Germany, the demonic activity was not as apparent as I had witnessed in other parts of Europe. The evil at work in this deceived nation was a more subtle and sinister kind.

When we got into Berlin, the Secret Police kept an eye on us from the first moment we got off the train. We had to go register at the Gestapo office, and every time we preached, we had to get a new permit. Usually the pastor would go down and sign for it. That way the police knew exactly where we were, and they could plant informers in every one of our services.

In those days, they didn't have miniature recording equipment, but the undercover agents were very fast with shorthand and would write down everything we said. Of course, we weren't political, so there wasn't much to report. Unlike Soviet Russia, it was not illegal to talk about Jesus — Hitler hadn't gotten around to that, yet. The government didn't hinder us as far as holding church services, but we couldn't preach on the street.

Quite a few of the German pastors in whose churches we ministered believed fervently in Hitler. It was hard for me to understand. They would sit for hours and talk about how wonderful their Fuhrer was.

Some would explain how Hitler had gotten rid of the gypsies and other undesirables and soon would clean the Communists out. Insisting he had stabilized the German government, they thought he would soon stabilize all of Europe.

They especially liked how he had moved against the Catholic church — and particularly how he had come against the Jews, whom they considered to be rich and dishonest. Some church people were members of the Nazi party, wearing brown shirts and Nazi insignias. It was frightening.

I'm a very sensitive person and so was Brother Carter. When we saw the front of Jewish-owned buildings blasted out by hooligans, we wanted to weep.

I remember vividly our last Sunday night in Nazi Germany.

As we were leaving to catch a train from Berlin to Denmark, the pastor who was taking us to the station said, "Brother Carter and Brother Sumrall, I know you took up a good offering tonight."

"Yes," we replied cautiously, knowing he was a sympathizer of the new Socialist government.

"I can't let you take it out of the country. Our government will not allow German currency to leave the Third Reich. At the border they will take it away from you, anyway, so why don't you give it to me?"

Before I could say, "No, we'll spend it on something at the railroad station," Brother Carter said, "I think that's a good idea. Brother Sumrall, please give him the money his church gave us."

I reluctantly handed it all to the pastor.

"Oh, thank you very much," gushed the man. "Hitler needs it. This is very nice of you to bless him."

Just as we were about to get on the train, Brother Carter stopped to buy a stamp for a postcard. He was always sending postcards to friends. He had written one to his brother John in England, and he said to me, "Oh, I'd like to mail this before I go into Norway. I'd like for this card to come from Germany, but I need a stamp."

"Yes," said the preacher. "Do you have any German money left?" He knew we didn't. We had returned it all.

Brother Carter said, "No, I don't have any German money."

"Do you have any American or British currency?" asked the pastor.

I cringed, but Brother Carter reached for his wallet. He pulled out a British pound note worth about $5 in American money.

With a big smile, the preacher said, "I can change British pounds into German marks."

I was so angry. The man had all our money, but he couldn't come up with the two or three cents to buy a stamp. Instead, the man's eyes just twinkled at the thought of getting $5 worth of British pounds sterling.

I wanted to speak up and tell Brother Carter that we'd be in Denmark soon, that he could just mail it there — but Brother Carter was so gracious. He handed over the pound note.

The preacher said, "I can give you marks for change, but since you can't take it out of the country . . . ."

So, he gave Brother Howard the pennies needed to buy a stamp — and kept the pound note.

Later, I asked, "Brother Carter! Brother Carter, why would you do that?"

"The Bible says if they ask for it, give it to them," he answered. "The Lord will give us plenty."

Brother Carter had such a beautiful spirit. I have never met anyone else in the world like him. And, as usual, Brother Carter was right. God did abundantly supply our needs, but I often wondered what happened to the pastor.

Before long the Nazism of Hitler was the only religion allowed in the "new Europe." The Protestant churches were shut down, and even the Nazi collaborators were imprisoned along with other Protestant leaders. I don't know that any of the pastors we had met survived.

Those pastors who had not defended the Jews and had turned a deaf ear to the Catholics were now the persecuted. When Hitler sent them off to work in coal mines, iron mines, and salt mines, they found out what happens when you put your trust in someone other than Jesus Christ. They had been terribly deceived by the powers of evil.

I found demon possession to be very common in Europe. Constantly I found myself in confrontation with the powers of darkness. Hundreds of people were set free, but I wasn't looking for any of it, didn't want any of it, and wasn't even telling anybody about it.

At the same time, I learned that I couldn't close my eyes when oppressed and possessed people came to my meetings needing to be set free. They would disturb the meeting, and I would come against the demons. God would deliver them, and in the process, thousands of people saw and were convinced of the power of God — and got saved.

I certainly had no interest in making this the trademark of ministry. Upon returning to the United States, I did not want to see handbills advertising the coming of "Lester Sumrall, the demon chaser." I didn't want that kind of reputation.

I remember thinking, *So, they have that Oriental disease in Europe, too. I hope God gets me out of this place.*

As I neared my twenty-third birthday, I realized I was not only older but much wiser than the teenage preacher of a few years ago. I was becoming quite a minister of the gospel, having been trained well by Brother Carter.

Upon returning to the States, I thought, *Thank God, I'm back in America now. I can just preach Jesus and have a good time and that's it.* I was afraid my ministry would suffer if word got out in America that I had been casting demons out of people all over Europe and Asia.

While visiting St. Louis, a local pastor asked me, "Would you come over and preach for me?" So I did on a Sunday morning.

In the afternoon he asked, "Would you go with me to pray for one of our church members?"

I said, "Yes, I guess so."

As we entered the humble little frame house, I saw a man, twenty-six or twenty-seven years old, sitting in a rocking chair and staring with a blank expression on his face.

His mother was kneeling beside him and saying, "Oh, son, speak to me. Speak to me."

Looking into his face, I saw something strange in those eyes. I said to myself, *I've seen this before — in Java and China and Japan and Europe!*

I sprang like a tiger across that room, grabbed that boy by the sides of his head, and said, "You unclean spirit, you come out of there!"

I looked at him and said, "I set you free by God's mighty power. Speak to your mother right now."

He turned to her and said, "Mama, I'm so sorry that I've acted like this. Would you please forgive me, Mama?"

When I asked how he had gotten into this condition, he told me he had gone to a seance to communicate with the dead. Although he'd been reared around Christians, it apparently hadn't rubbed off on him — any more than growing up around my mother had automatically made me a born-again believer.

He told me he didn't know what had happened, but during the seance he just went crazy. Later, his mother found him on the porch of their home. His clothes had almost been torn off of him, and he was bleeding as if he'd had a sound beating.

For six months he had not spoken a word of any kind. His behavior had also become very bizarre. If someone put his arm up, he would leave it up for twenty-four hours without getting tired all the while staring straight ahead. His family had to feed him and move him everywhere. Wherever they put him, he stayed until they got back, just as if he were dead.

When I left the house that day, the young man was walking around the room saying, "Oh, thank God. I'm going to live for Jesus, I'm never going to go back to spiritualist meetings, I'm never going to give myself to the devil. I'm always going to live for God. I'm always going to serve the Lord. I'm so glad you came."

He was completely and miraculously set free by God's power.

So I sighed to myself: *Well, they not only have this trouble in the Orient and Europe, they have it in America, too.*

I didn't know what to do, but I was still glad to be back home.

When I visited my parents, I received the surprise of my life. Seven years had passed since I'd been back home.

My father said, "I'm saved now, and I want to preach." He had given his life to the Lord.

I don't know how it happened, and nobody ever told me. He didn't fill me in on the details, but I could see that he had changed. We didn't hug or recount the "good ol' days," but it blessed me to know that my father wanted to live for the Lord.

He traveled around preaching until he got older. Then he went to live with my brother Houston while my mother was out holding revival meetings with my sister, Leona.

My father and I were reconciled, but we were not destined to grow close — even as adults. Of course, I loved him. When he wanted to travel as an evangelist, I even bought him a car.

He died a Christian, in Mobile, Alabama, on the beautiful Gulf that he loved.

I look forward to spending eternity with him in heaven.

He was my daddy.

13

Going in Different Directions

After only a few weeks in America, I became restless to return to the mission field. I was delighted when Brother Carter suggested we visit missionaries in South America.

First, we traveled across Brazil, where we had another brush with death.

On a three-day journey on a heavily laden freighter carrying logs to the timber mill, Brother Carter and I were sailing up the coast of Brazil from Joinville to Santos. The first night out, fierce winds whipped the South Atlantic into watery mountains and canyons. Our 100-foot ship bobbed like a peanut in the monster waves.

Billows began to break over our ship, and sea water poured through every crack of the decrepit vessel. Our cabin filled with twelve inches of water. As we bobbed and tossed about, I watched my hat and Bible floating back and forth across the room, but it was all I could do just to hold onto my bunk. Everything that wasn't secured was hurled from side to side.

Suddenly the captain burst into our room. "You! You're the preachers! We're sinking! Pray!" he ordered.

We did pray and, after six more harrowing hours, the storm slowly subsided. As day dawned, we were still afloat, but barely under way. We limped into port for repairs.

That night, my mother had seen a vision of us at sea. She went to her church and began to intercede urgently. A Baptist preacher saw the light on and came to the door. Stepping inside, he saw Jesus standing beside her. He fell to his knees in amazement and prayed with her, fervently pleading for our safety.

Then he went to his own church and prayed all night in the grove behind it. Finally at dawn, the Lord gave him assurance that we had been spared. He returned to my mother's church, found her still travailing before the Lord and told her, "Your son is all right. God has spoken to my heart. Go home now."

We had been delivered again.

Brother Carter and I ministered throughout Brazil, then from Bolivia to the ocean. We then headed back across the Atlantic to France, Spain, Portugal, England, back and forth across Europe, holding crusades wherever we went.

It was 1939, and Europe was gearing up for World War II. As Hitler's tanks invaded Poland, Europe became an increasingly dangerous place for those who lived there — and fields ripe unto harvest for the gospel. People were scared. They looked to God as never before.

In England, I was privileged to make friends with that legendary giant of faith, Smith Wigglesworth, the renowned author whose writings are used as college texts today. He had a miracle-studded ministry and the faith of Elijah. I met him when he was in his eighties.

He told me much about his life and ministry and the secrets of his great faith. He spent much time reading the Word of God, once issuing a challenge to anyone who could catch him without a copy of the Bible on him.

At one point I asked him why I never saw him down

Dr. Howard Carter and myself in Poland. We preached from city to city for three winter months. We don't look very comfortable, do we?

Treading through very difficult paths in Central America, visiting villages, towns, and tribes by muleback.

On my first missionary trip to Java, with Howard Carter. We are surrounded by Javanese gospel workers. I am second to the left, Brother Carter is fourth from the right.

March, 1936, Wilma, Poland. Brother Carter is in the center, with the beard that he grew in Tibet, and never did take off until the day he died. I am sitting next to him on his right.

Howard Carter and myself on our first missionary trip around the world.

George and Betty Sumrall.
My father and mother.

When I first started preaching at age seventeen.

Below left: Taken when I was around eighteen years old. I was ministering in Green Forest, Arkansas at the time.

Below: The greatest influence on my life, and one of the finest Christians I have ever known — my mother, Betty Sumrall.

This is my brother Ernest with his wife. Ernest lives in Mobile, Alabama. He pastored the great Stone Church in Chicago for 28-1/2 years. His grandson, David Sumrall, is pastoring our church in the Philippines.

Just completing an air journey around the world with Pan American Airlines, many years ago.

My beautiful bride and I on our wedding day.
September 30, 1944

In the Philip-
pines, standing
in front of our
home with Frank
and Steve. That
was many, many
years ago.

My wife and I are arriving at the Baguio Airport. Greeting us are
children from the Baguio Orphanage, which was the first one
with which we became involved.

Clifton Erickson and I were holding an outdoor revival in the Philippines. This is one of the huge crowds we had across from the City Hall in Manila.

I believe this is a 1952 Plymouth station wagon. I took this with me when we went to the Philippines to live and minister. It was brand new, and when we left I gave it to a missionary family.

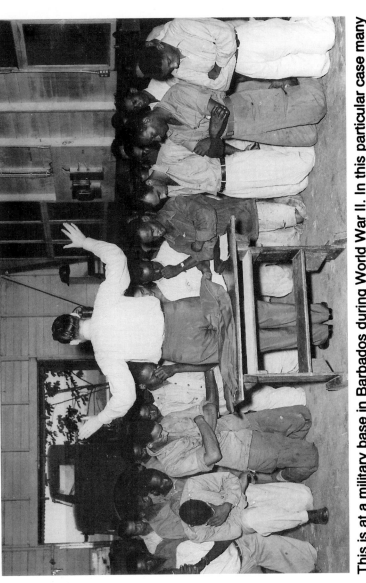

This is at a military base in Barbados during World War II. In this particular case many of the native people of Barbados gave their hearts to the Lord. I am leading them in prayer.

This is in the 1950s when we left for Hong Kong to build a church there. I am standing in front of a map, pointing toward Hong Kong. We later opened the New Life Temple Church in Hong Kong.

This was taken in Thailand while preaching there. In the background are bull elephants that pull logs and do the daily work in that country.

Peter, Louise, Frank, myself, and Stephen.
A portrait of the Sumrall family while pastoring in Hong Kong.

In Hong Kong we rented large billboards at the entrance to the ferry. Approximately one million people a day used this ferry. I am standing next to the billboard advertising New Life Temple, our church in Hong Kong.

This is the famous Jewish author, Sholomash Ogg and myself. We became very good friends while in Israel. He wrote famous books like *The Nazarene,* and others. We visited quite often. He was a very nice gentleman.

I'm speaking at a crusade in Brazil,
with my interpreter on the right.

This is the church I started in Manila where David Sumrall (my great-nephew) is now the pastor. I was there holding special meetings for a week.

My wife and I were welcomed back to the Philippines after ministering on a trip to the Orient. They put these leis on you like in Hawaii. Notice that she's pretty thin from the Philippine heat. As you can see, it didn't seem to bother me any.

Some of the first orphans that we adopted in the Philippines area called Baguio. We didn't adopt them into our family, but we adopted the orphanage and began to support it.

Left: The Sumralls at the ground breaking for radio station WHME-FM, South Bend, in 1968.

Below: This was our home in South Bend for many years. We gave that property to the church. They moved the house and made it into a girls dormitory, and this is now part of the church grounds.

This is the first church that I ever pastored in South Bend, Indiana. It seated 167 people. This picture was taken during a revival we were holding. It was indeed a special and exciting time in my life.

Pat Robertson and I at our first TV station, Channel 40 in South Bend, Indiana. He came over to help us with a telethon.

When we bought Channel 40, we had no set and very little money. We needed something for a sound barrier on the walls. I went to a poultry house and asked them to give us some egg crates. That's all egg crates turned upside-down on the wall behind Louise and myself.

This is the first church that we built at South Bend, seating about a thousand people. This is the Bible class on a Sunday morning.

My friend Kenneth Copeland and me.

This is one of the very first cameras we purchased for our South Bend station. God told me, "Unless you get on television and reach this nation, it cannot be saved." We are currently on the air twenty-four hours a day on this station.

In Vietnam they were very gracious to me. Since I was a writer and author, they took me all over the country in these combat helicopters.

We very often go into a country like South Africa, Zimbabwe, or Liberia, and set them up in the book business. We send them about $25,000 worth of merchandise, and then we take local money in exchange for it and buy food for people.

I was in Miami at one of their state prisons, preaching to the prisoners. They were very kind and attentive. I gave them quite a few books and videos so they would continue to learn about Christ.

A scene from the tragic fire which completely destroyed our TV station in South Bend.

One of the saddest days in our ministry was when our television station burned in South Bend.The entire station was burned to a crisp. Here they are picking up what is left and taking it to the dump.

My son Steve and I are cutting the ribbon for the opening of the new Channel 46 television station after the fire.

This is in Dr. Cho's church in South Korea before it was enlarged. It seats approximately 10,000 here. It now seats over 22,000. I am on the left with the interpreter on my right.

This is the famous football player, Rosey Grier, appearing on television with me.

In front of the camera on one of the new sets at Channel 40.

Our Feed the Hungry truck taking food to victims of Hurricane Andrew.

In a boat on the Sea of Galilee, two young men we admire very much. Rod Parsley on my left, Ucf Ekman on my right.

Doug Weed, former assistant to President Bush, and I in the lobby of the TV station in South Bend.

This is the ship, *Spirit*, being loaded. It has seven decks and holds five thousand tons. That's ten million pounds of food we are capable of carrying.

Our current church in South Bend — Cathedral of Praise.

Inside Cathedral of Praise. It seats approximately 3,500 people.

The C-130 on one of its first missions, delivering food to Nicaragua.

The Sumralls

Left: Stephen, Leslie, Steve, Rachelle, and Diane holding Arielle.

Right: Angela, Peter, David, Andrew, and Susan holding Adam.

Left: Lester, Frank, Amber, and Carol.

or depressed. He said that when he got up every morning, he never asked Smith Wigglesworth how he felt, but praised God, danced before Him, and looked to the Word of God for His direction and response.

On my final visit with him, Smith Wigglesworth told me, "I am going to bless you with my spirit."

We knelt, and he placed his hands on my shoulders and prayed: "God, let the faith in my heart be poured into the heart of this young man — and let the works that I have seen You do be done in his life and ministry. Let the blessing that You have given to me be his. Let the holy anointing that has rested upon my life rest upon his life."

I knew then that a new dimension of power would be evident in my life and ministry. I learned much about faith from Smith Wigglesworth, but the greatest benefit of my association with him was the spiritual impartation that has remained with me and shaped my life and ministry.

World War II's brutal aerial Battle of Britain had begun, but I was busy raising up three new churches in England that are still there today. I also became quite friendly with the British intelligence service, which kept close tabs on foreigners who traveled frequently into countries now occupied by the Nazis.

Did they think I was a spy? I certainly had done a lot of suspicious traveling back and forth. I'd traveled inside Nazi Germany and met with Nazi preachers. Now, many of the countries I had visited were occupied or under siege.

I took the opportunity to witness to the British agents whenever they quizzed me. They finally decided I was too religious to be a Nazi.

While soldiers marched and guns roared and Europe fought the early years of World War II, I planted indigenous churches and helped them become national organisms to bring Christ to the nations. However, I did this alone. Howard Carter was needed back at the Bible college in London. The war was causing great hardship, and he was needed at home.

When Poland fell and as Belgium, Luxembourg, Holland, Denmark, Greece, Hungary, Romania, Bulgaria, and France fought desperately for their freedom, British authorities became concerned about foreigners traveling inside their country. I was notified by British authorities that it was time for me to go home. All American civilians with temporary visas were ordered out of the country.

As the Nazis set Europe aflame, I had a heavy heart. I did not like having to leave Brother Carter. As he saw me off, we did not know if we would ever meet again.

I returned home alone and saddened. It was a time of adjustment to be back out on my own again.

Then in the fall of 1940, in South Bend, Indiana, I heard a missionary to Alaska weep as he told how difficult it was to reach the tough, independent people who lived in alcohol-seeped isolation there. He said frozen Alaska was the hardest place in the world to win the lost because the people were so hard and callous to the gospel.

I was inspired. I had survived drunks in Australia and gunfights in Arkansas, so I told him, "I'll go."

After taking a train to Seattle, I boarded the *S.S. Princess Norah* for Fairbanks, Alaska.

One starry night, the crusty old captain and I were standing on the afterdeck. I felt the Lord telling me to do battle for this old man's soul.

I turned to him and asked, "What do you think of Jesus Christ?"

Removing his pipe from his mouth, he looked at me in surprise, then gazed up at the twinkling sky. "Those stars are my god, young man," he said. "They have done more for me than anything I know. Since I was a small boy, I have lived on the high seas. Night after night, those wonderful stars have guided my boat. They have never led me astray. To me, they are the most beautiful sight in the world. I admire them, perhaps even worship them."

"But who made your sparkling gods up there?" I

asked. "Who organized and superintends them to guarantee that they stay in place to guide you?"

"I don't know," he retorted. "And I'm not sure anyone else knows either."

As he leaned over the rail, I said, "Captain, my God made your stars."

He grunted and did not reply.

Sometimes we are called only to plant the seed of the gospel. I pray that somebody else watered it in that fine old man. When I get to heaven, I'm going to look around for a certain grizzled sea captain.

I stopped in Prince Rupert, Canada, for a week of meetings, then bought a ticket to continue my journey. Before my boat sailed north, a pastor excitedly told me that a beautiful young missionary from South America by the name of Miss Louise Layman was arriving just an hour after my boat was to leave.

Unfortunately, I would miss her.

As I boarded my ship, her name lodged in my mind. I remember having the fleeting thought that it might be nice to meet a young, single, woman missionary.

I discovered that Alaska was no longer a land of long-bearded sourdoughs with a lust for gold dust. Nor was it a howling Arctic wilderness. Crisscrossing the beautiful interior by small airplane, I saw some of the most picturesque, but difficult and dangerous terrain in the world.

I preached in churches, clubs, radio studios, and school classrooms. I flew to frozen Nome on the Seward Peninsula in the Bering Sea, only a few hundred miles from Russia.

In Fairbanks, I preached in the largest public hall available. Since I had recently witnessed what was going on in Russia and Nazi Germany, I spoke strongly against their godless philosophies and leadership. I told what I had seen — the closing of churches and Christian schools and the takeover of businesses. I spoke of the anti-Semitic hatred and what I feared would happen to the millions of

Jews in Europe. I expressed concern about the welfare of our Christian brothers and sisters in those countries.

Suddenly, four or five men in the audience stomped out, scraping their feet, knocking over chairs, and slamming the door.

I felt something very sinister in their actions. I felt it so strongly that the next morning, I went to the local FBI office and talked to an agent about what I had seen.

He told me that he was, in fact, trying to locate some Nazis who were broadcasting shipping routes and troop movements across the North Pole to Germany. If Nazi Germany had ever decided to attack America, it could very well come across the North Pole. He said he was trying to trap those Nazis and asked if I would cooperate.

"How?" I asked, incredulously.

"Announce in the newspaper and on radio that you are going to preach another blistering sermon about Hitler and Nazi Germany."

That's what I did. Sure enough, the same men showed up, but this time they tried to disrupt my service by drowning me out with insults and jeers. When I would not shut up, they noisily stomped out again. To my amazement, the FBI agent I had talked to joined them, yelling insults at me, knocking over chairs, and slamming through the door with them.

The next day, he called me from his office and apologized. He said, "When we got outside, the Nazis took me as a friend and enlisted my help. They even took me to their headquarters. Now we have seven of them in custody — as well as their radio. Thank you for your cooperation. Sorry about the insults."

I chuckled. "No problem," I said. I had endured taunts and insults for Jesus many times. That was the first time I did it for my country.

On my way home by train, I stopped for gospel meetings in British Columbia, speaking in the towns of Terrace, Smithers, and Prince George. In each, I kept hearing about this lovely Louise Layman, that pretty, young missionary from Argentina — and the rich blessing that she had been wherever she went.

I became even more curious to meet her. She sounded like quite an intrepid missionary. What kind of courage had brought a young woman up into Canada during the winter? Normally, only zealous male missionaries brought the gospel here.

I wondered if I would ever get to meet her.

14

Long-Distance Romance

The United States was hurled into World War II when Hitler's allies, the Imperial Japanese military launched a sneak attack on Pearl Harbor on December 7, 1941.

With thousands of other loyal American boys, I rushed down to enlist in the Navy. I was told that as a twenty-nine-year-old preacher, they might use me as a chaplain, but that they didn't need any just now. I was told to keep in touch.

Disappointed, I turned to spiritual war.

I decided to travel in the only part of the world not yet touched by the war — Mexico and Central and South America. There I confronted the evil source of all wars, Satan, who hates man and lusts for blood and violence against the beloved beings created in God's image.

I did not know that Hitler's agents were trying to enlist Mexico's help for an invasion of America up through Mexico — reclaiming for Mexico their hard-fought but lost possessions of Texas, New Mexico, Arizona, and California.

The Lord guided me away from the Mexican capital

and other large cities where anti-American sentiments were strong. Instead, I was led to Mexico's remote highlands where I ministered to Indians back in the forest — people who had never seen a watch or a camera. I had a tremendous time teaching them about Jesus.

I learned a lot about humility, eating their food and learning to respect their heritage while showing them the love of God. One of their favorite meals was a jungle stew — made from a whole bird, including beak, feathers, toes, and everything in between.

After two and one-half months, I ventured into the Central American Republic of Guatemala.

There I was distressed to see the state of Christianity. For four hundred years, the descendants of the Mayans had practiced a form of Christianity that only resembled the Catholicism forced on them at swordpoint by the gold-hungry Spanish conquistadors. Those invading hypocrites had taken entire peoples into slavery, giving them a choice between death and converting to Christianity.

Well, it won't work that way. The result was terrible resentment against the white man's God, a mish-mash of native tradition, and not the best of Catholicism.

I found that most of the natives didn't know a thing about salvation. They went to mass and there lit candles to the old Mayan demon-gods.

I accepted an invitation from missionary Perry Dymond to preach for six weeks further south in the poverty-stricken republic of El Salvador. We traveled from hamlet to hamlet in what, even today, is the most backward and strife-torn country in the Americas.

It was the rainy season, and the tropic jungle seemed impenetrable. We climbed steep, volcanic mountain trails on mule back — reminding me of my time in Tibet and China. But this was the rain forest, the lair of vicious jaguars, poisonous vipers, wild boar, brilliantly colored birds, and all kinds of monkeys — some we saw and others we only heard screaming in the distance.

It was almost dark when we came into the village of Las Delicias, made up of a half-dozen huts. I wondered where any congregation would come from. But around seven-thirty that evening, out of the jungle came several hundred men, women, and children. They gathered in and around a crude church building built by a native Christian leader named Señor Gutierrez.

Dying with a high fever, he had heard the salvation message and accepted Jesus as his Lord. He was not only saved but miraculously healed. He had been so close to death that his family and friends had already made his coffin.

When he built the gospel hall in gratitude to Jesus, he hung that coffin on the rafters. There it still hung as a silent testimony to the power of the true God.

I stood behind an improvised box-pulpit at one end of the room, and the Indians pushed inside, packing the place beyond capacity. Many had walked for miles to hear me. Those who could not get inside began singing Christian choruses outside.

It was a powerful service with several delivered from demons and many saved. At the close of that meeting, the people lighted torches and started their long, dangerous treks back through the jungle to their homes. The blazing lights kept the animals away and provided light for their feet on the mountain trails.

In my mind's eye, I can still see them leaving — single-file on the narrow paths up the side of the mountains, their torches turning into distant pin-pricks of testimony as they sang songs of Zion. I was reminded of Psalm 119:105: "Thy word is a lamp unto my feet and a light unto my path."

My journey continued south into Nicaragua, then Panama, Colombia, Venezuela, and Brazil.

In the back country of Brazil, I was traveling by bus. At a small town, it stopped to let off passengers, and there in front of the bus station I saw a man tied to a pole.

He was a mad man. Like an angry animal, he lunged at his tormentors and screamed obscenities. The man was large, almost naked, with long, unkempt hair. He was filthy from having lived in the dirt like an animal. Children threw things at him, while the adults stood back and laughed. The people said he had no family. He was dangerous, so they had tied him up as a public spectacle.

As our primitive bus bumped on down the red dirt road, I continued to relive that scene. That night as I preached, I could not forget that man. He was a human being, and yet he was not. He possessed an immortal soul, but a demonic spirit now controlled him. He had a God-given right to be free and normal, but he had been reduced to the level of a wild animal.

Only the devil could find joy in such a sad situation.

In spite of what religion seeks to teach and its inability to resolve the emotional needs of this generation, it is a confrontation like the mad man at the bus stop that makes me quote Hebrews 13:8: "Jesus Christ is the same yesterday and today and forever."

Did I go back and pray for that man? No, I was a foreigner on a bus in the middle of nowhere — en route to a speaking engagement. I prayed that the Lord would send somebody to set that poor man free.

There were so many dramatic encounters that I do not have room to recount them here. I met Christian men and women — giants of the faith — in the jungles and mountain villages, many who lived in victory amid terrible poverty and persecution.

On I went into Peru and Paraguay. I visited leper colonies and prisons, as well as the homes of the mighty and the forgotten. I saw llama herds in the Andes Highlands and breath-taking vistas, beautiful rivers, waterfalls, and lakes.

Wherever I went, I was intrigued and inspired by the faith of Christians and the terrible darkness of the unsaved.

I had seen some of these people in my vision of the nations when I was a young man.

By December 1942, I had preached from Alaska at the top of the Americas to beautiful Argentina at the very southern tip.

I did not know it, but the war had already touched Argentina. Here, too, the Nazis had strong sympathizers in the government, which toyed with joining Hitler's Axis but stayed neutral until the last days of the war. They threw their support to the Allies only after Hitler was on the verge of defeat.

It was in Argentina that I saw a truly beautiful sight that would change my life. I was invited to a wedding, and playing the bridal march on the church organ, was a young lady who literally took my breath away. As I studied her, she turned and looked directly at me. For a brief instant, we smiled at each other.

I had to know her name.

Discreetly, I asked one of the local pastors who had invited me.

"Oh, she's a missionary from Canada," he said. "Her name is Louise Layman."

I was stunned.

This was the courageous girl missionary I had heard about on my way to and from Alaska. I thought, *Right there's the girl I would like to marry.*

I got the pastor to introduce us.

During the wedding reception, I was able to talk with her and was astonished that we had so much in common. We had many mutual acquaintances. Conversation with her was so easy!

Before that encounter I had just about decided that I was destined to be a bachelor. I had no special gift with women. Indeed, I was wary of getting too involved with anybody who would require a commitment to settle down. I had a world to evangelize!

I had molded so much of my life and ministry after

my mentor, Brother Carter — and he had no time for sweethearts.

Neither had I — until now.

Louise asked what I had thought of her native British Columbia. Later she told a friend that she could tell from the "light in my eyes" that I had loved the beautiful, rugged North.

As she and I talked, she confessed that she had heard about me, too.

Our second meeting was on Christmas Day at a mission in Henderson, a town about seven hours by train from Buenos Aires, the Argentine capital. I had been invited there to preach and was pleasantly surprised to see her.

This, she explained, was her mission base. When I was invited to her pastor's house, I was astonished to find a beautifully wrapped parcel from her under the Christmas tree with my name on it.

I opened it and found a little wooden burro with wheels under his feet. When in motion, his hips went up and down in a comical fashion. I promptly named it *Luisa*, her name in Spanish.

From Henderson, I traveled up the Plata River, then the Paraguay River to Asunción, the capital of Paraguay, then on to a mission to the Lengua-Moscoy Indians. Riding on horseback and primitive river boats, I had plenty of time to meditate on this wonderful girl I had met.

I wrote her a note of appreciation for the hospitality I had been given on Christmas Day in her pastor's home. I told her how I had inked the burro's name on its wooden back and had given it to a missionary child. Dutifully, I gave her the name of the new owner and the location of the animal's new "stall."

She wrote me back. I was thrilled beyond measure. I was almost thirty years old, but I felt like a giddy schoolboy. Rereading her letter became a daily high point of my life.

I wrote her again, and she responded. In our increasingly frequent correspondence, we found that we had so much in common. We were born the same year, the same month, and only eleven days apart. We had both accepted Christ as our personal Saviour while in our teens and had promptly offered our lives to Christian ministry.

In our letters, we discovered we had both ministered to congregations while still in our teens. From the first days of our conversions, we had both yearned to do missionary work in foreign lands. We had both left our parents' home in North America to answer our calls and had departed for mission fields in the same month of the same year — she to Argentina, me in search of Howard Carter.

I found out that after we had missed meeting each other by an hour in British Columbia, she had stayed in the very guest room I had occupied. There she had found a hand bill flyer with my picture on it advertising my gospel meetings.

Upon returning to Argentina, she had been surprised to hear on the short-wave radio a series of sermons that I had recorded. The announcer of the station, HCJB, "The Voice of the Andes," broadcasting from Quito, Ecuador, introduced me as "Evangelist Lester Sumrall, the world-traveled revivalist and author." He said that the station would be broadcasting a series of my sermons three times a day. She had tuned in regularly.

When it was announced that I was coming to South America, she wondered if I would be coming to Argentina. However, the itinerary that was reported said nothing about my coming there.

She said that she had still wondered if she would get to meet me.

I was flattered beyond measure.

After two years of constant correspondence, it was only appropriate that if I were to ask her to marry me, that I should do it by mail.

She accepted — also by mail!

The day I received her glorious, wonderful letter, I made this entry in my journal:

> I am engaged today! One month and three days after I wrote my proposal, the answer was received. Sitting here in the great Pan American air terminal in Mexico City, waiting for the plane to take me to Tuxpan where I shall go back and visit the Otomi Indians, I read again and again the letter received this morning from Louise, forwarded to me from my home in Chicago.
>
> She has consented to leave Argentina and return home to Canada where we shall be married later this year.
>
> May God unite our lives to do a great work for Him in every part of the world. She said she had prayed about the matter for a week and had consulted her senior missionaries on the field.
>
> The long string is about to knot. My heart feels certain she will make a fine companion as she is the choice of God and my choice.
>
> My total bank account is five hundred dollars. I wrote a check on it, adding twenty-four dollars in cash and dispatched a draft by airmail to bring home the one I have chosen.
>
> The distance is so great and the war restrictions and censorship so slow, it takes time for word to come and go. I trust the same censor read both letters and knows how it all came out!

Three months later, in May, she left Argentina to come join me. At New Orleans' International Air Terminal, I waited, both nervous and excited. This would be only our third meeting.

When her plane did not arrive, I was a mass of frustration and energy. I was beside myself. I prayed fervently for her safety and felt the Lord's gentle assurance that all was well.

It was not until the next evening that her name appeared on the passenger list of an arriving plane. Even then, immigration authorities would not release her until some American citizen stood responsible for assuring she would cross the States and continue to her native Canada.

Of course, I was more than glad to take her off of the immigration officials' hands. We embraced and I whisked her away in my green Hudson coupe.

After Louise arrived home in London, Ontario, Canada, my green Hudson became quite well known in the district. I held meetings and crusades all around Michigan and Ontario so I could be near her.

She was no slacker — accepting quite a number of invitations to speak as well. One weekend put us in competition when she spoke in Sarnia, Ontario and I was holding a crusade across the St. Lawrence River in Port Huron, Michigan.

The months between May and our September wedding will always be remembered in our lives. They were months of making memories, months of building companionship that would brave the difficulties and challenges of a missionary life together.

They were months of romance, months of becoming tenderly acquainted, time for talking over the future and of planning for years of combined ministry. They became months of synchronizing our two distinct personalities. I was amazed how closely our ideals were paralleled. Everything seemed divinely planned.

We could see God's hand and His divine schedule leading us in separate ways while preparing us to unite in a lifetime labor for Him.

We were married on September 30, 1944. It was one of those beautiful "Indian summer" afternoons, a perfect day for a wedding. At 2:30 p.m., I stood facing the audience as the organ played the familiar strains of the wedding march.

I was a typical bridegroom — my pulse racing as I saw my beautiful bride walking down the white-carpeted aisle on the arm of her stepfather, the Rev. J.D. Saunders. I added my gasp of appreciation to the other audible whispers of "Isn't she a beautiful bride!"

My brother Ernest was my best man. Officiating was Dr. C.M. Wortman, missionary physician and uncle of the bride.

At the close of the ceremony, Mrs. Wortman sang "Together with Him," a song that was especially prophetic of the life we were beginning together.

Our union was pronounced, the wedding reception was celebrated, and farewells were said.

My shiny green Hudson roared away in the twilight of the lovely Ontario countryside, rich in autumn's glorious colors. Our destination — Niagara Falls, the honeymooners' haven.

We were both thirty-two years old.

15

Where Do I Go from Here?

My new bride and I had many invitations from churches across Canada and the United States to minister as a team in special meetings. Indeed, Louise was just what my services needed — the touch of a preacher's wife.

She sang so beautifully. In fact, I could listen to her all evening, but, of course, people expected me to preach.

Together we sought the Lord as to the direction our lives were to take as man and wife. Were we to hold crusades across the South as I had in my teenage years? Should we try to rejoin Brother Carter?

The world was still at war. Travel out of the Western Hemisphere was difficult, if not impossible. The tide was turning in the favor of America, Great Britain, and the other Allies, but terrible battles were still to come — the fire-bombing of Dresden, the buzz-bomb attacks on London, the landing at Normandy, the atom-bomb destruction of Nagasaki and Hiroshima.

We sought the Lord and searched our hearts.

God proved to be our unfailing guide and directed our hearts to set off on a honeymoon missionary tour.

We started out traveling through Quebec and New Brunswick then ventured into rugged Nova Scotia. The poor, rural families with whom we often stayed made makeshift beds for us in their kitchens near the stove.

As we preached to the fishermen and their families, we found that the people of these Canadian Maritime Provinces had been grossly neglected by most religious groups.

In December our itinerary brought us back to the United States for a great New Year's youth rally in Detroit. Then, while Franklin D. Roosevelt was being inaugurated for his fourth term, we were on our way to San Juan, Puerto Rico, in the Caribbean.

En route, we ministered in Cuba and Haiti. After arriving in Puerto Rico, we visited indigenous churches, propagated by their own people without the presence of even one resident missionary. These Christians, however, faced intense spiritual warfare. Many respected Puerto Rican doctors, lawyers, and politicians boasted of their involvement in spiritualist cults that conjured up demons for miraculous healings. Witch doctors were constantly sought out for exorcism — using "good spirits" to drive out bad ones. We found ourselves constantly confronted by demonic spiritual counterfeits.

Living conditions were poor and we found ourselves sleeping in houses infested with roaches, fleas, and bed-bugs. The thick swarms of mosquitoes had no mercy. As a result, Louise contracted a fatal form of malaria. An American-educated doctor held out little hope for my lovely bride.

Grief overwhelmed me, and I got down on my knees and prayed like I'd never prayed before, asking God to miraculously heal and strengthen her. And that's just what He did!

We continued on our journey throughout the West Indies and South America, up Brazil's Amazon River for a thousand miles. In spite of the millions of mosquitoes,

Louise did not have a single recurrence of malaria. We rejoiced in God's goodness.

While visiting the vast Waller Field Air Base in Trinidad, West Indies, Louise and I celebrated our first wedding anniversary. The missionaries, soldiers, and Christians of the island put together quite a party for us. I received a stuffed crocodile, and my wife was given a beautiful tray made of varicolored, inlaid wood.

From there we flew back to South America, ministering in Guyana, then Surinam, and on to Brazil, where we spent our second Christmas as man and wife preaching on street corners. Wherever we went — whether to lone individuals or to the masses in great crusades — we witnessed to the love and mercy of Jesus Christ.

We made our way south overland through Uruguay, then to Buenos Aires, Argentina, where Louise had labored for eight years. We conducted a successful crusade in a rented auditorium there. We preached in Chile, then Peru, Ecuador, and the Panama Canal Zone.

In Guatemala, we deplaned long enough to rush over to the church there and speak before returning and heading for New Orleans.

Now what were we to do? What did the Lord want of us? We had traveled 50,000 miles on a glorious honeymoon in which thousands of souls were saved — but what was next?

The war had ended.

The entire world was open to us, it seemed.

Then, Louise gave me the most joyous news of our new life together: She was expecting a baby!

A baby!

My heart jumped, and my mind raced. A baby? We needed a place to call home. I couldn't haul an infant through the jungles — could I?

We bought a little house in Springfield, Missouri, which became our headquarters for the next eventful months as we continued speaking throughout America at conventions, camp meetings, and missionary conferences.

Our first son, Frank, came ten days earlier than the doctors had predicted. My mother and sister were staying with my wife, and I went up to St. Louis to preach at a special meeting between Christmas and New Year's Day.

On the morning of December 31, my telephone at the hotel rang at 7 a.m. Picking up the receiver, I heard my sister declare, "We've just taken Louise to the Hospital. She's going to have the baby right now."

I shouted, "I'll be right there.

Without checking out of the hotel or packing my things, I tore downstairs. My car was parked right in front, but in my haste and excitement, I hailed a taxi and ordered the driver to speed me to the airport — that I had to catch a plane.

"My wife is having a baby!" I declared to the ticket agent. A plane was going to Springfield in ten minutes, she said calmly, but it was filled.

"I want to take that plane." I exclaimed. "I'll stand in the aisle if I have to. Sell me a ticket!"

Calmly, she shook her head. "You'll have to be standby."

"Sell me a ticket! Don't talk to me!" I shouted. "My wife's having a baby right now. Right NOW! Don't talk to me — sell me a ticket!"

"Well," she hedged. "We overbooked that flight."

"Don't talk to me," I pleaded, "SELL ME A TICKET!"

So, she did. I went and got first in line so I was the first one on the plane. It's not very far between St. Louis and Springfield, but it seemed an eternity to me. I wanted to go up to the cockpit and tell him to "step on it, Buddy!"

I did manage to stay in my seat until we touched down, then jumped off of the plane and hailed the first taxi.

I got to the hospital before my wife came out from the anesthesia. Aside from the doctor, I was the first one to hold the newborn.

Oh, what a beautiful baby! He was so handsome — with a little round head. I thought he was absolutely lovely.

Frank was born in Springfield, Missouri, on December 31, 1946 — just in time for me to be able to list him as a deduction on that year's income tax return.

I was almost thirty-five years old.

And we were so happy!

I had asked the Lord to give me sons so they could enter the ministry. I told Him that I didn't want any lawyers, doctors, or anything else. I just wanted preachers.

In fact, throughout our children's young lives, my wife and I very carefully planned for their future. We never talked about my ministry. We always talked about the family ministry. They grew up knowing and firmly believing that my ministry was also theirs. Preachers should bring their whole family into the ministry — just as they would if they ran a family farm or were a commercial fisherman.

My advice to preachers is: Don't leave the kids at home. Teach them by taking them with you. The Bible says that God appointed Aaron to be the high priest and from that time on, the high priests were Aaron's sons and grandsons and great-grandsons.

When God anoints a man, He very often puts it in his blood. In this country, most Christians don't understand the priesthood at all. I have heard things such as "I've had a hard time in the ministry and don't want my boys to be pastors."

I was determined not to be like some preachers I had known who didn't pay any attention to their kids.

Shortly after Frank's arrival, I had an invitation to return to Europe. Although I wanted my family to come with me, Louise knew that little Frank was too small for such a trip yet. She said the two of them would stay at home and pray for my safety, for souls to be won to Christ

— and for my quick return.

Aboard the *R.M.S. Queen Mary*, I sailed for Southampton, England, where I was stunned to see the devastation. Brother Carter's Hampstead Bible Institute in London had sustained repeated direct bomb hits, destroying the facility.

My reunion with him was joyous. Although he had escaped serious injury, the emotional stress on him and the people of England had been terrible. Many still seemed dazed.

I sailed to France and rejoiced to find a number of the churches and pastors whom I had known in better times. In Normandy, I wept to see the beach where our fighting men had landed and so many had died. Across Europe, entire towns had been erased from the face of the earth.

As I met with Christian leaders, the Lord began to urge upon me a plan for reaching the millions of unsaved more effectively. I began to realize that in most of the countries of the earth, a large portion of the population was usually concentrated in the cities. The Lord told me: "From 50 percent to 60 percent of all the nations in the world have only one big city. If you were to raise up a great evangelistic center in that major city, you could touch the whole nation for Christ."

I began to think about the countries where one city dominated the whole country. I thought about Havana, Cuba and Bógota, Columbia.

Manila in the Philippines particularly came to mind. About 80 percent of the business of that whole nation takes place in Manila. The government, the universities, and the businesses were all located in the city. Manila *is* the heart of the Philippines. The best students from throughout rural villages gravitate there to attend college, then they become lawyers, doctors, and businessmen in Manila.

I returned to the United States with a renewed vision and dedication. When I presented my plan to several denominational mission boards, however, they showed little interest in evangelizing the world's great cities.

"Brother Sumrall, it costs too much," I was told again and again. Their weak excuses and lack of vision infuriated me.

Then the Lord began to show me three things about reaching the nations for Him:

First, we had to bind the powers of the devil operating in the land. I had seen firsthand the need to shackle the powers of Satan and set people free before God's Word could be preached in power.

Second, new converts must be taught and nurtured in God's Word. The best missionaries are not visiting foreigners, but fired-up, empowered native evangelists burning with a desire to win their homeland for Jesus Christ — but first, they must be trained and grounded in the gospel.

Third, I saw the absolute necessity of going into the capital cities and the major metropolitan areas and building evangelistic centers. These centers would win the lost, feed the sheep, and send out hundreds and thousands of new leaders to win their kinsmen to Christ and establish their own churches.

The apostle Paul went to the great cities of his day. From there the nationals took the gospel out to the smaller towns and villages. If you remember, they set the world on fire.

I knew that if we operated this way, we wouldn't have to send foreign missionaries behind every banana tree. The key was to go to the big city of each country and then send the nationals out to their own people.

Burning with this vision, I sought the Lord about how to go about it. I was only one man, and none of the mission boards seemed to share my intense urgency. As I travailed before the Lord, I felt no answer. I was enormously frustrated, especially when God sent me in an entirely different direction.

While conducting a revival in Memphis, Tennessee, I received a totally unexpected request to pastor a small church in South Bend, Indiana. To be truthful, when the call came I wasn't very impressed. I couldn't think of any reason why the Lord would want a fired-up southern boy to settle down in such an obscure Yankee town in the snow belt of America.

Then, a second and a third request from the South Bend people finally sent me to my knees, pleading with the Lord to give me firm direction and leading. I wanted to set the world on fire for Jesus, not become the pastor of a small church.

The people from South Bend told me that they had fasted and prayed and that the Lord had impressed upon them that they should remind me that they needed me. I was puzzled.

I was a globe-trotting revivalist and author.

I had not toured the world with Howard Carter just to preach weddings and funerals at a tiny church in Indiana.

"What is going on?" I asked the Lord.

16

Your Fruit Shall Remain

N othing is more satisfying to a minister of God than to bear fruit. If he pastors a church, it grows; if he holds a revival meeting, people get saved. On the other hand, nothing is more devastating than to see no fruit coming forth. When your efforts are fruitless, you don't know what to do. You wonder if you're out of the will of God, if you're a personal failure, or if the devil is thwarting your progress.

I know a man who led a great revival — 100,000 people were converted. When I went to that country later and asked to meet the converts of that revival, nobody in the churches there knew where to find them.

"He didn't work with us," the church leaders told me. Apparently, the evangelist had left town the same day he finished the meeting.

"He didn't set up a new congregation. He just left with lots of movie reels to show his supporters back in America so they would keep sending him support. We wouldn't know where you could find twelve of his converts still following the Lord."

That's what happens when we try to do great things

for God in our own strength, in our own pursuit for success, or our own wisdom. Preachers and evangelists usually do what is good, but not always what is best.

We can start off with a belly full of fire, but if we don't listen to what God tells us to do, we will fall back on our own cleverness and gimmicks. That's when preachers start to fake the anointing and kid themselves that their ministry is valid.

There is no doubt in my heart that God had called me as a teenager and sent me out. He had promised me, "If I send you forth, you will bear fruit." His promise came straight out of John 15:16. The second part of that verse says, "And your fruit shall remain." The proof remains in the churches I started in schoolhouses across the Deep South years ago. They still exist today.

In Australia I started a church in a tent across from a bar. Today it has a thousand people. *Today.* Not a long time ago but right now. In England I started three churches. They're there now, today — living and growing and being blessed of God. *Today.*

In Alaska I started three churches. They're still going. In the Philippines there are a number of churches that I founded and built myself. In Hong Kong I established New Life Temple, and it has started two churches. All those churches are still functioning in the power of the Spirit.

When God makes a commitment to you, it is true. God will perform all He has said He would perform. Remember: God is in charge. He is God. *We are not.*

My life is a living witness that when God says something — believe it! It will work. It will function. It will come to pass. You can believe God! But you have to listen to Him.

If you misunderstand this, you will think that Lester Sumrall is full of pride — bragging about all the churches he founded.

That's not the point at all.

I'm telling you to seek the Lord before you try to do anything. I'm telling you that if you fail to do this and attempt to do great, noble things in your own strength, you will fail.

Why did my churches thrive? Because the Lord sent me out. Because I obeyed. But obedience is seldom easy.

Why should I go to South Bend? I wondered.

It was simple. I had to obey. Either God was in control of my life or He wasn't. I had to rest in His plan for me and not struggle to do things my own way.

That's why I had to accept that pastorate in South Bend when my own desire for world evangelism told me to go to the great cities of the world and set up evangelistic centers.

I had to obey — or fail.

I didn't want to go to South Bend. I knew my vision for great evangelism centers was valid, and that my yearning to reach the whole nation was from God.

When the Lord told me to go to Indiana, I pleaded with Him to let me do something else.

He answered, "You'll never understand My heart if you don't pastor. Evangelists don't understand My heart — but a pastor gets into the sorrows of the family and sees into the intimate relations of a home. He understands what it means to be a shepherd because I'm a shepherd. If you don't become a pastor, you're never going to understand My heart. I want you to go to a hard place."

God confirmed that the South Bend church was to be my training ground to accomplish the goals the Lord had set upon my heart.

It wasn't easy.

In early December, Louise and I and little Frank arrived at our new pastorate. We met in a small, miserable, run-down building with a low ceiling.

After I surveyed the situation, I advised the congregation that we should sell the building and start over. Not everybody agreed. They had been meeting together for twenty-six years. They had built that building themselves and loved it dearly.

Attendance ran somewhere between 50 to 75 adults and maybe close to 100 children. The building seated 167, packed and jammed. That left no room for growth.

Besides that, the building was decrepit.

Whenever it rained, the roof leaked. You couldn't keep it from leaking, no matter how much you worked on it. The cold wind blew right through the walls. If you walked near the wall, you would hit your head on the ceiling because the whole thing was out of plumb. The congregation had constructed the building using no architectural plans and with free labor and secondhand lumber.

I didn't want to preach in a place like that.

I told the people, "This little old building has to go. I can't stand it." So, I sold their building to a man who turned it into a print shop, which was a good use for it.

I wanted our new church building to be on Michigan Street, the busiest street in South Bend. An entire city block was empty at the time, but the man who owned it (and also owned a liquor warehouse and a car dealership) didn't want to sell it.

Fortunately for us, his mother came to our church. So I asked her to talk to him.

Then I went to see him at his office.

He said, "Mama's been to see me."

I knew he had a reputation in the community for being hard to deal with so I spoke very bluntly to him — taking spiritual authority in the situation. "She'll come and see you again if you don't do what I tell you to do."

He said, "Well, the cheapest I can take for it is $45,000."

"Well," I said, "I don't want to give you that much — but I'll give you $35,000. You have to take it."

He agreed without any argument and sold us the property. There was only one problem — I didn't have $35,000.

I said, "I want to tell you how honest I am. I am in the process of selling the church property, and I'm going to get $10,000. So, I'm going to give you the $10,000. Then, here's our deal: If I don't have the other $25,000 in say, three to six months, you can have the whole thing. I'll just leave town."

His eyes got big. He was an ungodly businessman and couldn't believe he'd gotten an offer like that.

"You'd do that?" he asked.

"That's what I said, and that's what I'll do."

We signed the papers and took the property.

Then I began to feel a little stupid. *How am I going to get $25,000?* I wondered. *I've never seen that much money in my life.*

Well, the Lord will give it to me, I said to myself.

Sure enough, it wasn't a week until the telephone rang and a man on the other end of town said, "You own a whole city block on South Michigan Street?"

"Yeah," I said, "what about it?"

"I want just a little piece of it."

"Naw, it's not for sale."

"What do you mean?" he yelled at me on the phone, "You're a dog in the manger. Why don't you come out of that manger and sell me a piece of that city block?"

I said, "Well . . ."

"How much do you want for just a hundred feet of it?" he asked.

"I'll take $30,000 maybe, I don't know," I answered. "But I won't take any of your arguing, I can tell you that."

He said, "Just let me make one offer — $29,000."

"You got the money in cash?" I quizzed.

He said, "Yeah."

"I'll have the papers drawn up and meet you at the courthouse."

The church only owed $25,000, so now we had $4,000 extra to start our building.

With part of the money, we bought a big tent and put

it up on Michigan Street. We held a crusade in that tent for eleven weeks. The church, Sunday school, the office, and all the records were moved into that tent.

A lot of people said, "We lost our church." But in our tent crusade on that busy street, we tripled our church's attendance.

At the same time, the Lord was at work providing the money to construct our new church building.

One morning, a woman came to our home. "I want you to know I don't like you or the way you preach," she said. "But God told me to give you $1,000 for the building fund and here it is."

So, I took her contribution.

An old man who lived across the street from our tent had a large, rambling house. He would sit on the front porch and rock in his rocking chair, listening to the tent meeting, but he didn't come across the street and join in.

One day he told a messenger, "Tell that preacher to come see me."

So I went over and asked, "Yes, sir, what can I do for you?"

"I want you to take me downtown."

I thought, *I'm having a tent meeting and trying to build a church and this man who doesn't even know me wants me to be his taxi and chauffeur?*

"I want you to take me downtown," repeated the man. "I don't have anybody else to do it."

I thought for a moment and said to myself, *Well, the Bible says to be a servant, and I'm getting to be one.*

"All right," I answered, but I was thinking, *With all the preachers in town, why don't you call on somebody else?*

So I got him in my car and asked, "Whereabouts?"

"Take me down to the bank."

I figured, *Well, he's got one of these social security checks, and he wants to get it cashed and I have to do it for him.*

So I drove him downtown and took him inside the bank. I sat in the corner kind of grumbling about this old man taking up my time. I was busy and had to preach that night.

While he was up at the counter talking to the teller, he turned around to me and said, "Preacher, you need any money?"

"Yes, sure do," I chuckled.

"How much would help you today?"

"Oh, a lot." I didn't know he had any money. He looked like he didn't have a penny to his name. He was an old man and lived by himself. He didn't even have anybody to help him keep the house clean.

"Would $4,000 help you?"

I came up off that seat. That was like $20,000 today.

I said, "Help me? Yes, sir!"

The bank teller handed him $4,000 in cash.

Then the old man turned around and said, "Well, this will help you today. Let's go back home."

He did that several times, and the day we dedicated the new church, he died. I preached his funeral. The day he finished his job of helping me build my church was the end of his life.

When winter came, it was too cold to continue meeting in the tent. Temporarily, we rented a third floor dance hall in a downtown building until the back part of our new church building was far enough along for us to move in. By summer, we were able to occupy our new auditorium, which could seat a thousand. We named the new church Calvary Temple.

Almost as soon as we moved in, Evangelist Rex Humbard walked in the door and said, "Can I hold a meeting here?"

I said, "You sure can."

His crusade was so packed that policemen had to direct traffic in the street.

Evangelists Clifton Erickson and Oral Roberts each came and we had colossal movements of God.

In Sunday school our attendance was up around 2,300.

Meanwhile attendance in our own family was growing. On July 27, 1950, our second son, Stephen, was born.

In South Bend, our outreach continued to grow. We had been able to buy ten acres of land and a modest parsonage on East Ireland, which then was a country road.

The Lord opened the door for me to take a six-week missionary trip to Europe, Israel, Egypt, India, and the Philippines. It was 1950, the year that I turned thirty-eight years old.

The highlight of the trip came during a three-day city-wide crusade in Manila, the Philippines.

This huge city, which was home to several million people, did not have one soul-winning church. There were, however, numerous missions out in the surrounding jungles.

World War II had been over for almost five years, but most of Manila's downtown buildings remained scarred from the long and brutal Philippine resistance against the Japanese who had invaded right after attacking Pearl Harbor.

The Japanese cruelty had been unprecedented — designed to crush the spirit of this nation that had fought courageously alongside the Americans. These were the islands to which U.S. Gen. Douglas MacArthur had made his famous pledge of "I shall return."

It was here that thousands of Americans had died and many more had been taken captive in the Battle of Bataan and the siege of Corrigedor in Manila Bay.

The Philippine national spirit had been badly bent but unbroken during five long years of resisting the brutal, often vengeful Japanese occupiers of their country. The Philippine people had suffered terribly, and a spirit of despair now enveloped them.

We rented Rizal Stadium and saw hundreds respond when we asked them to give their hearts to Christ. Afterwards, however, I was deeply burdened because we had to leave them without leadership or even a place to worship.

Not long after I returned to South Bend, we were conducting a missionary convention when the Lord spoke to my heart. I was reminded of my vision of the millions going down the highway to hell. I knew the Lord was saying to me, "Lester, will you go to Manila for Me?"

I asked the Lord if I could be released from my pastorate. The church had paid off its indebtedness.

The answer was affirmative. Furthermore, the Lord told us that in the Philippines, "I'll do more for you than I've ever done before."

"Oh, this is going to be exciting," I said to Louise, "If God supplied the needs of my ministry in South Bend, think what he's going to do in Manila."

In San Francisco our little family boarded the Swedish freighter *S.S. Wangaretta*, and it took twenty-two days to reach Manila.

"What?" You may exclaim, "You mean you took that little newborn baby, a toddler, and your wife off to the slums of Manila?"

Absolutely. In fact, my third son, Peter, was to be born in Manila.

Any husband who is called by God, according to the Scriptures, is called first and foremost to be the priest over his household. How could I leave my family behind and still be the priest of my home?

I believe fervently that a minister who does not minister to his family is setting himself up for heartbreak and shame.

How many times have you heard about a preacher's drug-pusher son or his disgraced daughter? That sort of thing brings shame to our Lord.

I wasn't about to let my boys become casualties of my ministry. As the priest of my home, I fulfilled my duties. That means telling the children Bible stories when they went to bed, hugging them when they lost their Little

League games, cheering when they won a ribbon in the Science Fair, and certainly, praying fervently for them.

As parents, we need to pray, when that child is still a toddler, that he or she will serve the Lord. We need to ask the Lord to send the right spouse for them — that's so important!

And don't forget that the family that plays together stays together. That's no misprint. Play with your children. Have fun with them.

I've taught all three of my sons how to play golf and how to swim. On Boy Scout camp-outs, I've taught them how to build a fire and keep it from going out or burning down all the other trees. I played basketball and tennis with them.

What pride swelled in my heart when they were good enough to win against me on the tennis court or in a good round of golf! Frankly, after years of letting them score points on me, it took a little adjustment on my part when, as grown men, they began holding back so they wouldn't beat me too badly.

My family had always been a big part of my ministry. God blessed me and gave them to me to nurture and raise. They were my children and no one else's. That's why I made time for them.

When it was their time, I didn't let anything else get in the way.

When I walked out of my office in the evening, I had to be finished ministering to my church. I shut the door and told all the problems that I'd be back tomorrow. It was time to minister to my family and give my wife and boys my full attention.

I didn't burden my wife with all the problems of the church. Over the years, I'd seen pastors' wives on the verge of nervous breakdowns, about to crack under the pressures of their husbands' ministries. Louise's job was to keep our home running smoothly. She didn't need to be loaded down with the troubles of every other family in the church.

When I got home, I didn't talk about the problems I'd faced during the day. Dinner was the time we listened to our three growing boys tell about everything they had done at school or at play. My wife and I would laugh at their antics and clap our hands at their accomplishments. It was a special time of sharing and encouraging.

Having three boys can be a real challenge, but we made it easy by teaching them to love one another. In fact, I've never heard my sons quarrel. Of course, they would get upset with each other once in a while, but they wouldn't speak harsh words or hold grudges.

They were a blessing to my ministry and became great little travelers. If I was going to be gone for a while, I would always take the entire family along. They were my responsibility.

When we went to Manila, I took my family with me. Later when we spent time in Hong Kong, they came along and had to adjust to a different culture.

It was an education that I just couldn't have them miss.

17

Filipino Time

We had quite a surprise waiting for us in Manila. Our contacts had rented an abandoned vegetable market in Tondo, one of the worst slums in Manila, about eight miles from the center of town. Our "church" was an ugly, open, iron-bar structure with walls made from dead, browned banana leaves woven into chicken wire. It stood next to an open sewer.

The first day of services, two bloated, dead hogs lay in the filthy ditch, covered with flies. The stench — even when we removed the dead swine — was unbearable.

The forty people present at the first church service had to cover their noses with bandannas. Twenty-five of the forty were students from a local Bible school. The others were visitors from outlying missions. No unsaved people were in attendance as far as I could tell.

If I had been disgruntled with the original South Bend church building, I was in despair over this pest hole. I was so discouraged that I didn't know what to do.

My heart was in the bustling, throbbing city. That was where the teeming millions of people could be found. Nobody was going to come out here. It was dangerous after dark.

I began to plead with the Lord for property in the middle of Manila on which to build the evangelistic center I had envisioned all these years. It was to be far more than a church. It would be the nerve center of a great evangelistic and training outreach to win the entire Philippine Republic to Jesus.

We all began to pray and ask God to give us some land — and He did. He gave us a wonderful downtown lot, two blocks from the National Congress. It was a perfect location — at one of the busiest thoroughfares in the city and not far from the central YMCA, the Red Cross headquarters, and the national offices of the American Bible Society. Furthermore, the lot had already been cleared for us by a World War II bomb.

With the help of friends back home in America, we raised the $20,000 necessary to purchase this choice property. The proud Filipinos, however, were wary of all foreigners and reluctant to admit their needs to Americans, whom they considered to be rich.

Since I had no building to house a congregation, I concentrated on learning all I could about the people, their history, and their customs. After all, Jesus had come down from heaven to identify with us and our problems. I could do no less for these fine people to whom God had sent me.

Among other things, I learned that they had a completely different concept of time. If we announced that Sunday school would begin at nine-thirty in the morning, the first people would begin arriving around eleven o'clock, with most getting there by noon.

I was frustrated but made every effort to adapt.

A local man tried to explain "Filipino time" to me one afternoon after he had missed sending off a friend leaving by ship. When he showed up a half-hour after the boat had pulled out of the harbor, I expressed my consternation.

He patiently told me, "Brother Sumrall, you must learn that here in the Philippines, we hurry very leisurely."

Indeed, many Filipinos felt that Americans were much too uptight about time schedules and were unnecessarily enslaved to clocks. They expressed it through passive resistance — by being consistently tardy.

Official channels were just as sluggish. If you needed a permit or building approval or blueprint in ten days, you could expect to wait thirty days before some low-level clerk rejected it because of some minor thing that could have been corrected when you turned it in.

Bribery was not merely expected, it was mandatory. There were professional brokers who, for an exorbitant fee, would help you bribe all the right people in order to get a permit approved. That irritated me — and as a result, all our permits and authorizations became ensnared in unending red tape.

Other customs, however, were admirable. For example, if you hired a Filipino worker and he decided to quit, he would send a cousin or brother to take his place.

Now that we had a location, we needed a building. God guided me to a disassembled B-52 airplane hangar stored in a large garage owned by the Pepsi-Cola company. Although the materials were worth about $50,000, we were able to purchase the whole thing for $10,000.

When we brought all the pieces of the hangar to our downtown property, the building materials covered virtually every square inch of our lot. We hired an excellent local architect to design an attractive front and interior. I envisioned a forty-foot cathedral dome, forty-foot steel and glass windows on each side, and a large sign over the entrance proclaiming "Bethel Temple — Christ Is the Answer." After all, we had to live up to the standards of our uptown neighborhood.

In the meantime, we made arrangements to hold a city-wide crusade at the San Lazaro race track. American evangelist A.C. Valdez, Jr. agreed to speak. We posted signs, distributed handbills, and took out an expensive ad in the *Manila Times* that went all over the country.

The opening service attracted about twelve hundred people. Each night the crowd grew larger until we were drawing about five thousand every meeting. At the close of each service, the aisles were filled as hundreds came forward for salvation. Then, we prayed for the sick until past midnight.

When we announced a water baptism for the final Sunday afternoon, thousands showed up. That afternoon, 359 men and women were immersed. Out of that group, our church in Manila was born.

Then we ran into major problems. City officials were not sure what to do with us. Here was a foreigner trying to put up a B-52 hangar in the middle of downtown and claiming he was going to turn it into a big Protestant church. I balked at paying bribes, and had no local political connections.

Furthermore, it did not help us that we were an independent group, while most of the officials were staid Methodists, traditional Catholics, or else Moslems, spiritualists, animists, Hindus, or Buddhists.

For six months it seemed I was just beating my head against a wall. I was sent from one office to another in a futile quest for the permits and approvals I needed.

I really was wondering if I had just missed God's instructions and should have stayed in America. My vision for a great Philippine revival just wasn't working out.

As I prayed about my frustration, the Lord spoke to me. "Who sent you?" he asked.

"You did."

"Well," he said. "I'll take care of you."

Then He did an incredible thing.

He sent us Clarita Villanueva, a jailed seventeen-year-old orphan daughter of a harlot and soothsayer.

We first heard about her on an incredible radio broadcast. "Good evening, ladies and gentlemen," intoned the announcer. "If you have a weak heart, please turn your radio off."

I had a strong heart. I had to if I was going to endure the official red tape piling up around my ears.

Reaching for the radio dial, I turned up the volume. Suddenly, a series of nerve-rattling screams blared through the radio speaker, followed by the sound of absolute pandemonium. "Help me, help me," shrieked a young girl's voice. "They are killing me."

In the noisy background, voices of men could be heard through the chaos: "This can all be explained . . . ." "I believe we are looking at epilepsy . . . ." "Delusions and hallucinations are often . . . ." "This child is suffering from nothing more than extreme hysteria."

I could hear others saying, "She is blue in the face . . . ." "Look, there are new teeth marks on her neck." There were shouts of "Look at that!" then the terrified, tormented screams of the girl again. Such a haunting, horrible scream it was — the scream of a girl possessed by the devil. I had heard those screams so many times before.

The announcer was broadcasting from Bilibid Prison, and said that Clarita Villanueva, a young, provincial girl in the prison, was being attacked by invisible demons.

She would have been dismissed as mad except that twenty-five witnesses, including the Manila Police Department's chief of police, testified to seeing the horrified girl suffer inexplicable bite marks before their very eyes.

I leaped up and found myself standing in the middle of the room.

"Louise," I exclaimed, "that poor girl is demon-possessed. That's exactly the kind of thing that I told you about in Java, China, Europe, and even in America. It's horrible. Honey, try to get some sleep. I'm going into the front room."

I lay down on the floor and began to weep before the Lord for that tormented child. I couldn't get out of my ears the sound of her blood-curdling shrieks and pleas for help. I asked the Lord to cast out the devils and deliver her.

Early in the morning, God impressed upon my heart that I was to go to the prison where He would use me to deliver her and bring great revival to the Philippines.

At first I strongly objected to the idea of going to the prison. But the announcer had said that doctors, scientists, professors, legal experts, and even spiritualists had tried to help her to no avail.

I turned the radio back on. The announcer told how Clarita, a seventeen-year old, had known a life of tragedy. She did not remember her father. He died when she was very young.

Her late mother had been a harlot who made extra money as a spiritualist and professional fortune teller, holding seances, communicating with demons claiming to be the dead, and using clairvoyance to predict to clients what they could expect in the future.

When Clarita was about twelve years old, her mother died, and the girl became a street child. Local harlots in Manila became her teachers. By the time she was seventeen years old, Clarita was a regular in the bars and taverns of Manila.

One morning at 2:00 a.m. on the streets of downtown Manila, Clarita had made the mistake of offering sex to a plainclothes police officer. She was arrested and taken to Bilibid Prison, a three hundred-year-old building now used as the Manila city jail. It had been built by the Spanish colonists and used by the Americans, then by the occupying Japanese as a place of interrogation and torture.

Two days after Clarita was incarcerated, the street harlot began to be bitten severely on her body by something invisible and unseen. There seemed to be two of them — a huge monster-like thing and a smaller one. They sank their fangs and teeth deep into her flesh, making bloody indentations. They would bite her neck, back, legs, and arms simultaneously. Blood flowed, mostly underneath her skin, from the bites. The seventeen-year-old was being driven insane — and the experts could not explain what was happening.

When the girl was taken to the prison hospital for observation and treatment, the doctors declared they had never seen anything like it. The strange attacks occurred daily, baffling all who saw it.

I turned off the radio and knew I had to go to the prison.

The next morning, all the newspapers were full of the sensational story. A Dr. Mariano B. Lara was permitting anyone with any kind of legitimate credentials to view the phenomenon. Filipino, Chinese, and American doctors, university professors, and other professionals were trying to analyze the situation.

Even the editorial cartoonists that morning had drawn pictures of the entities from Clarita's descriptions. United Press International and other world news services began to report the story worldwide. One news account said that when a doctor had accused the girl of putting on an act, Clarita had glared at him and said, "You will die."

Reportedly, Dr. Manuel Ramos had been outspoken in his disbelief in the supernatural nature of the phenomenon. He made sport of the entire idea before others and stated that the entire thing was some kind of hoax.

According to witnesses, he and Clarita had a confrontation in which she told him he would die. That same hour the next day, the doctor expired without showing any signs of illness. The coroner attributed his death to a heart attack.

As I read the accounts, I realized that this had been going on for about three weeks. The newspapers also told of a jailer who suffered the same fate earlier. They said Capt. Antonio Ganibi, the chief officer of Bilibid had become irritated with the girl when she crawled under his desk — and there, claimed that the demons were tickling her.

She would laugh boisterously when he told her to

come out and would move her body as if someone's fingers were moving over her body. When she finally came out from under the desk, she asked the captain for a small, metal crucifix that she normally wore on her dress.

"Captain Ganibi," she reportedly asked in a low, whining voice, "where is my crucifix?"

"I don't know," he reportedly responded.

She looked back under the desk where she had been, then said, "Look in your pockets. Maybe you have it."

To satisfy her, the captain turned both his pockets wrong side out. He replaced his pockets and as he did, the demon-possessed girl looked at him in a strange way and with her whining voice said, "Captain, look again!"

He felt a cold shiver go up his spine and, as he put his hand back into his pocket, he touched the metal crucifix. He handed it to the girl, and she told him he was going to die, just like Dr. Ramos had.

Indeed, Captain Ganibi became sick and he reportedly "wilted like a flower before the sun" and died. Nothing was ever found organically wrong with him.

The large demon, Clarita said, was a monster in size. He was black and very hairy. He had fangs that came down on each side of his mouth. The doctors verified her description by the teeth marks on her body.

The smaller entity was almost like a dwarf. He would climb her body to bite her upper torso. Both spirits liked to bite her where there was a lot of flesh, like the back of her leg, the back of her neck, the fleshy part of her upper arms. They would bite deeply into her, leaving ugly, painful bruises.

Reportedly, Dr. Lara and his medical assistants had called in all sorts of observers, medical doctors, surgeons, psychiatrists, and professors from the Far East University and the University of Santo Thomas. No one had any solution to the problem. Reportedly, many were worried about who would be the next victim of her curse.

Dr. Lara and his staff, according to the newspaper, had sent out word to their international colleagues everywhere. Three thousand telegrams came in, mostly from Japan and India, telling them what to do with invisible biting monsters — but not one Christian had any solution to the problem.

Supposedly a local group of spiritualists had examined the girl and said it was John the Baptist biting her.

That morning, God told me, "If you don't go, I don't have anybody else."

That's the first time I knew that God needed *me*. It gave me a good feeling.

I said, "Now, listen, if You don't have anybody else but me, I'll go for You, even though I don't want to go."

I got into my car but, since I didn't know where the prison was, I decided to visit my architect friend. Although he also owned a shoe factory and was a millionaire with a magnificent home, I found him to be a very amiable person.

I asked him, "Have you heard about the girl bitten by the devil?"

"Oh, I've followed that in the news. Man, isn't that exciting?"

"I'm going to go pray for her."

"I'll go with you." He was a Catholic and didn't know what he was getting into. He just wanted to see a crazy woman.

"Do you know the mayor?" I asked.

"Oh, sure, he often swims in my swimming pool when I have parties. He and I are very good friends."

I said, "Can you get into his office without permission?"

"Sure. The mayor has a private elevator into his inner room and I can go straight through there from underneath the city hall." In that great city of millions of people the city hall is about two blocks long and about four stories high.

So he drove right up underneath the building. We went into the basement and got into a secret elevator that opened up right inside this huge office. The mayor, seated at an oversized desk and surrounded by about fifteen or twenty people, was signing papers.

A mayor's office is a hectic place, especially in a Third World country where everybody wants a friendship thing from him. He had a stack of papers in front of him, but at the same time he was talking with all these people.

An enormous man, over six feet tall with a size-19 collar, he had been a guerrilla fighter in the Philippine resistance during the Japanese occupation. He knew what it was to run through the mountains and fight with a machine gun hanging on his neck.

My friend said, "Arsenio," that was the mayor's first name, but the mayor didn't pay any attention. He was talking with all these people and signing those papers.

The architect repeated, "Arsenio." They were friends, but he didn't even look up.

Finally my friend said, "Arsenio, here's the man to cast the devil out of Clarita."

Suddenly, the mayor's pen left his fingers and slid clear across the desk. The mayor stood up and said, "What? What? What?"

"This American here wants to go to the prison and pray for that girl. Can he get your permission?"

The mayor walked around and, towering about a foot over me, put his hand on my shoulder and said, "Don't you know that a doctor is dead and that the head jailer is dead? I don't want an American to be the third one."

I said, "Oh, I'm not going to die. God spoke to me and told me to cast the devil out of her so she'll be healed."

The mayor of this enormous city looked me over and asked, "You won't get hurt now? I couldn't afford to let an American get hurt. This is a national situation, and I don't want it to get international."

I said, "Mr. Laxon, I won't get hurt. I didn't want to come, but Jesus told me to do it." I flipped open my Testament and read to him from Mark 16:17, "They that have faith should cast out devils."

I said, "Jesus said that."

He had never seen it. Of course, he didn't know a thing about the Bible.

He said, "Is that true?"

"Well, Jesus said it."

"You won't die if you go over there?" he asked.

"No," I said. "I won't die."

"Well, then go," he agreed.

"I'm willing, if you're willing."

He said, "I'm willing," and he told one of his assistants, "Call Bilibid Prison."

18

Bitten by Devils

I t took us about half an hour to get to the prison on the other side of Manila.

Once inside, my architect friend and I searched for the head doctor. When we found him, he was in the morgue with two cadavers. Wearing a rubber apron, he was trying to figure out how they had died the night before.

He demanded "What do you want?" kind of belligerently.

"I've come to pray for Clarita Villanueva, the girl who is being bitten by devils."

At first he got angry at the notion that demons were to blame.

I recounted my experiences in Java and Europe, which seemed to impress him. He listened as I told him Clarita was possessed by a demon and that I could help rid the girl of her tormentors.

In total seriousness, the physician told me that in his thirty-eight years of medical practice, he had performed more than eight thousand autopsies and had never found a demon in any of the corpses.

I nodded politely.

I decided it was not the right time for a complete doctrinal explanation of the nature of Satan and his demons or the theology of deliverance. Instead, I suggested that the doctor would witness a powerful display of God's power over evil.

He nodded seriously but did not look convinced. I realized that I needed to convince Dr. Lara that I knew what I was doing and that I knew how to help this girl.

I began slowly, "Dr. Lara, there are only three powers in the universe. There is the 'Positive Power,' or the power of a creative and benevolent God. There is the 'Human Power,' or the power of men here on the earth. Then there is the 'Negative Power,' or the malevolent and sinister power of the devil. These powers are real and evident around us. Now, do you think Clarita is acting under God's power?"

Dr. Lara shook his head slowly and replied, "No, not God's power."

"Then do you feel that, with your experience with human beings, she is acting like any human being?"

"No, the actions of this girl are not related to human beings."

"There is only one power left. She must be acting under demon power!"

Dr. Lara then explained that his broad experiences as a medical man had not prepared him for this encounter with something that was beyond a doubt — "supernatural."

I continued, "Dr. Lara, if there was a 'negative' force in the universe over which a 'positive' force had no control, our universe would go to pieces. If there is an evil that no right can correct, then evil is mightier than right. This cannot be. If this girl has demon power in her, then Jesus Christ can deliver her from that power."

Then I read from Mark 16:17, " 'And these signs shall follow them that believe — In my name shall they cast out devils.' Do you believe this?"

Dr. Lara looked at me and said, "I believe. Now who will help us?" He explained that the chaplain of Bilibid Prison, the Catholic bishop of the Philippines, and the priests at the Catholic healing center at Baclaran had all refused to pray for her — therefore, he had assumed that assistance from the Christian community was not an option to be explored further.

He turned to me and said, "Reverend, I am humble enough to admit that I am a frightened man."

I said, "You found Clarita, and you may be next."

He nodded, a worried look on his face.

I opened my Bible again and said, "Let me read something to you." I turned to Mark 16:17 again, "And they that have faith shall cast out devils."

"Who said that?" he asked.

"Jesus. Those were the last words he ever said before he went to heaven."

"Oh, oh." He had never read it in his life. "Well," he said, "if Jesus said it, it must be all right."

I said, "Oh, yes, it's all right."

He asked, "Can you do it?"

I said, "Jesus can do it. He said, 'They that have faith.' I have faith."

"Oh," he replied, "let's go do it."

Let's go do it. How did he get in on it? I was so tired by now, working my way through that Manila traffic, getting to the architect, getting to the mayor, getting to Bilibid. It was about ten-thirty in the morning already. I was tired. It was May, the hottest month of the year in Manila.

I said, "I'm too tired. I'll be back tomorrow morning at eight o'clock and do it."

I requested that no medication be given the girl during the time that I was praying for her, and that no other groups be permitted to pray for her or to offer assistance in any way until I was finished. If Jesus healed her, He was to have all the glory.

Dr. Lara agreed. We set the time of prayer for the following morning at eight o'clock.

I had not eaten since the night before, so I laid down on the floor in a closed room and fasted and prayed all day. By the next morning I hadn't slept now in two nights and had not eaten in one day and two nights. I felt the mighty spirit of God.

The following morning I arrived at Bilibid Prison. Upon entering its dreary walls, I felt like there was going to be a contest between the God of Elijah and the prophets of Baal — and the observers would know if the Lord be God.

Bilibid, with its centuries of bloody history, was to witness a new kind of battle. Here, the Spaniards had imprisoned their victims. Here, the occupying Japanese had conducted uncounted atrocities. Here, American prisoners of war had almost starved until their liberation by Allied troops. Behind its walls were hundreds of criminals who had broken the law. To say the least, it was an uninviting place.

After our meeting the day before, the doctor had called all of his friends — policemen, doctors, university professors, the press — and he had about 125 observers. When I got there and saw all those people, I said, "Hey, all I wanted was to just pray for her."

He said, "If you're going to do anything, you're going to do it before all of us. The whole world knows about this, and you can't do a thing without us seeing you."

I said, "Well, in that case, let's go."

Leaving the main part of the prison, we walked across to the women's section, more than a city block away. I was accompanied by the architect of our church, who was a Catholic. Dr. Lara brought with him a professor from the Far Eastern University.

When we started walking toward Clarita's cell, I saw all these people that Dr. Lara had invited. I felt like a mouse in a house with a hundred tomcats.

Suddenly, I began to doubt. I didn't have a chance. I didn't know what to do.

In that brief moment of fear and doubt, the devil said, "Now, you will make a fool of yourself!"

I silently rebuked him in the name of Jesus.

As Dr. Lara and I led the way down the dusty prison road through the barbed wire gates by the sentries on duty, I glanced back at the motley crowd. Obviously, I was going to be the day's big story.

At the request of the press, we did not go to Clarita's cell. Instead, we went to a small chapel near her cell. The chapel had steel-barred windows and a plain Catholic altar at one end of the room. It was a dreary and barren place.

After we all gathered in the chapel, Dr. Lara commanded that Clarita be brought in.

He asked me, "Do you need some incense? I can get it for you."

I said, "Well, I'm just not sure what I might need. You just stand by."

He said, "All right."

As the girl entered the door, she observed each person slowly and closely.

When she came to me, her eyes widened, and she glared at me saying, "I hate you!"

These were the first words the devil spoke through her lips to me — but I had never seen her before, and she'd never seen me before. The Spirit of God rose up within me.

I suddenly felt great compassion for this petite seventeen-year-old who had been with many men, sometimes eight or ten a night. She had been abused and beaten and kicked around like an animal since she was twelve. Now the demons had bitten her so many times that the tooth marks could be seen on her skin .

In an attempt to shock me, the demons within her began to speak curses at me, to curse God, to curse the blood of Christ, and to declare rude obscenities. Apparently they did not know they were dealing with a former delinquent street brawler who had heard every dirty word before. I was not even startled.

She did this in English — yet days later I had to converse with her through an interpreter, since she could not speak English.

I had her sit on a wooden bench, and I drew a chair up in front of her. "Clarita," I said. "I have come to deliver you from the power of these devils in the name of Jesus Christ, the Son of God."

Suddenly, the girl went into a fit of rage. She screamed, "No! No! They will kill me!"

I grabbed her beside her head on both sides. I didn't know that when a male touched her the monster would bite.

They had to let female nurses touch her, because when a man touched her she would get bitten.

When I laid my hands on her, that thing bit her on the side of her neck. It had sunk its fangs in deep and blood was running. It was a filthy mess. Then, she fainted.

Her body became rigid, and she became unconscious.

She had done this before when the doctors had tried to talk with her — baffling them completely.

The main doctor spoke up and said, "We'll have to quit now. When she gets unconscious, she's that way for three or four hours."

I was so angry by this time I said, "No, we're not going to quit."

When she fainted away, I caught her and held her chin up and said, "You come back!" Suddenly, that thing came through like a lion, raging. Raging!

The doctors looked at one another and said, "It takes us three or four hours to do that. How did he bring her around in thirty seconds?"

This was spiritual warfare, not natural medicine. I had dealt with devils before and understood some of their antics.

Taking hold of her head with both hands, I cried, "Come out of her, you evil and wicked spirit of hell. Come out of her in Jesus' name!"

She immediately began to rage again. With tears flowing down her cheeks, she begged me to leave her alone. Then she showed me the terrible marks on her arms and neck where she had been bitten that moment.

There were the terrible teeth marks so severe that some small blood vessels underneath the skin were broken. Rather than feeling like quitting, I went into the greatest battle of my life.

I have never known anything like it.

The devils would curse God, and I would demand them to quit and tell them God is holy. Then they would curse the blood of Jesus, and I would rebuke them, reminding them that He is the Master over every evil power and that His blood is holy.

They cursed me in the vilest language, declaring they would never leave. It seemed that the powers of darkness realized they were in deadly conflict.

Indeed, this was more than a battle for Clarita Villanueva. With the press gawking behind me, I knew this was a battle for Manila and all of the Philippine Republic. I smiled, knowing that Jesus would win.

Finally, it appeared that the girl was delivered. The devils did not talk to me anymore or bite her.

Many of those present thought she was delivered, but I knew in my spirit that she was not. It was nearly noon, and I was soaked with perspiration and nearly exhausted.

When I looked around, I saw several people with tears in their eyes. They had been moved by the great battle.

I told Dr. Lara that I desired to go home to fast and pray, but that I would return the following morning. He agreed.

My visit, of course, was the day's big story. The

headline in *The Daily Mirror* the next day read, " 'The Thing' Defies Protestant Pastor." Here is an excerpt of the story:

> "The Thing" and a Protestant minister, Dr. Lester F. Sumrall, were locked in a struggle to the finish at the chapel for women detainees at the city jail this morning. . . .

I spent the rest of the day in communion with God. It was precious. I could feel God's presence hovering over me, urging me not to be afraid.

That night, Pentecostal missionaries Rev. Arthur Ahlberg and Rev. Robert McAlister visited me at home and offered to come with me the following day and stand between me and the crowd to keep them from getting too close during prayer.

I thanked them for their support.

I didn't pick up the architect the next day. I didn't need him anymore, and he didn't know what it was about anyway.

Upon our arrival at Bilibid, the captain of the prison said that Clarita had not been bitten that night. But I knew she was not delivered yet.

This became evident when the devils saw me. Through her lips they cried, "Go away! Go away!"

I sat on a small chair in front of her and spoke back with a feeling of authority, "No, I am not going away, but you are! This girl will be delivered today!"

Then I requested every person present to kneel — including the press. There were as many present as the day before, perhaps more.

I warned them not to mock or laugh for when the devils came out of Clarita, they might attack another victim.

Doctors, newspapermen, police officers, prison officials, and professors knelt as I prayed.

The battle began again. The devils realized it was their last struggle. They cursed and cuddled their victim, but the extra day of fasting and prayer had made a difference.

Finally, I felt the release that they had departed. Clarita relaxed, the demon look departed from her eyes, and she smiled.

I looked around and saw newspaper men who had been weeping. There were tears in the eyes of doctors, too. Hard-boiled jailers were openly crying.

I began to sing softly with Brothers Ahlberg and McAlister joining me. The second time, the others joined in the refrain:

> *Oh, the blood of Jesus,*
> *Oh, the blood of Jesus,*
> *Oh, the blood of Jesus,*
> *That washes white as snow!*

I asked Clarita if they were gone and she said, "Yes."

"Where did they go?"

"Out of that window," she responded, pointing toward the steel-barred window.

We were ready to depart when suddenly, like a flash of lightning, the devils reappeared. The girl screamed.

I cried to them, "Why have you returned? You know you must go and not return."

Speaking in English through her lips, they replied, "She is unclean, and we have a right to live with her."

I answered them in a determined voice, "Mary Magdalene was unclean with seven like you, and Jesus came into her life and she became clean by His mighty power. Therefore, I order you now to depart. Jesus has made her clean."

They lacked power to resist. They left, and she became normal again. I explained to her what had happened and got her to pray with me for the forgiveness of her sins.

Again, she seemed all right.

As we were preparing to leave, the same scene was repeated.

This time, I was very upset.

I ordered the demons to tell me why they had returned. They spoke in English through her lips, "She has not asked us to go. She wants us. It is only you who desires for us to leave."

Again I demanded that they leave her. Clarita told me they were gone through the window. I explained to her why they returned and told her to tell them to leave and never return. She did.

Then, I led her in prayer, pleading the blood of Jesus against them. It was about noon. Clarita was weak from the ordeal. I told the prison officials to let her rest and to give her food.

As I was leaving, I said, "Clarita, I am sure these devils will return again. After I am gone, they will come. Then you must order them to leave without my being present to help you. You must say, 'Go, in Jesus' name,' and they will obey."

With that, I left the prison compound.

That evening at eight o'clock, Clarita called to the guard on duty, "Mr. Pangan, my fingernails are very long, may I borrow your pocket knife to cut them?"

The guard replied, "I would like to, but prison regulations are that no prisoner shall be permitted to have a sharp instrument."

The guard, who had watched the deliverance, offered, "But I will cut them for you — come here."

Before he could cut two nails, Clarita let a blood-curdling scream, "Help, they are back to get me! They are standing behind you!"

The scared guard jumped up and watched what he said was the greatest struggle he had ever seen. He could not see the aggressors, but he could see the girl in mortal combat screaming hysterically. As she cowered, she cried to the guard, "What did the American minister tell me to do? Tell me quickly!"

The guard cried back, "Say, 'Oh, God, deliver me in Jesus' name and in Jesus' blood.' "

Clarita screamed these words at her invisible enemies and, as she did, she lurched forward and grabbed with her hands something unseen.

She went into a coma.

The prison authorities who were in the compound gathered. They laid her on a table, but her hands were clutched tightly.

When the doctor pried her hands open, to his uttermost astonishment, she was clutching strands of long, black, coarse hair. It was in the palm of her hand and under her fingernails.

Dr. Lara placed this hair in an envelope and put it in a guarded place. Under the microscope, Dr. Lara found that the hair was not from the head, nor from any part of the human body.

I personally saw this hair under the magnifying glass. It was about two inches long, coarse, had no root, and showed no signs of having been cut.

The doctor had no answer to this mystery. How an invisible being, presumably a devil, could have lost hair by little Clarita pulling it out is one of the strangest facts of this case!

19
The Miracle that Changed a Nation

After Clarita was healed, the doctor got so excited, he rushed me over to the mayor's office and said, "Oh, my God, Mayor. My God, Mayor. You've never seen anything like it. We heard the devil talk. We heard him rage. We heard him cuss. Oh, my God, this man healed that girl. This biting business will never happen again."

The mayor came over and hugged me and said, "What can I give you? I can give you anything you want."

I said, "I've been trying to get some blueprints signed in your office for several months. The officials want palm money. I don't have any. I don't belong to any denomination. I just don't have any."

He got mad and his face got red. He bellowed out at one of his assistants. They brought in the blueprints and he personally put the stamps on and handed them to me.

He said, "If you ever have any trouble in this city, let me know because I will take care of you."

From that time on, if I went into a restaurant to eat and he was there, he would jump up from the table and hug me in front of everybody.

Unfortunately, after Clarita's deliverance, I did not take time to speak to the newspapermen. In fact, I asked them not to write about the incident. Even Rev. McAlister went to them for me and requested they not publicize the event. They retorted that this was a big story and that their readers had the right to know its conclusion.

Since the Methodist Church is the oldest Protestant church in the islands, the press assumed I was a Methodist and wrote it in the papers. In many of the articles, what they said was not completely correct. I feel responsible for this since I didn't permit them to interview me and left the city the next day for the country to get away from the publicity.

My picture was on the front page. One of the headlines read, "Devil Loses Round One." They thought there would be fifteen rounds. The local newspapers, magazines, and radio stations, told and retold the story of Clarita's deliverance in sensational and often exaggerated detail. One headline read, "He dies — the devil is dead!"

The *Manila Chronicle* announced: " 'THE THING' IS DEAD! This every believer can now proclaim as Clarita Villanueva claimed yesterday that 'The Thing' has finally been exorcised.

"The girl said the prayers of an American minister, Dr. Lester F. Sumrall, who purposely visited her to purge the devil, did it."

Upon my return to the city the following week, Clarita had been before Judge Natividad Almeda-Lopez in the Court of First Instance in Manila.

In a calm and collected way, she testified, "Since last Friday, the day the American missionary prayed for me, the devils have not returned!"

Judge Almeda-Lopez placed Clarita in Welfareville, an institution for wayward girls, for observation.

With Dr. Lara, I went to visit her twice. Overjoyed at our coming, she rushed to greet us, saying she feared she would never see us again. We sat and talked with her at length.

While at Welfareville, we asked permission to conduct a religious service for the two hundred girls living there. This was granted, and several days later a group of musicians and singers from our church went to the institution for a service. Clarita was the center of attraction and we did everything possible to make her feel welcome.

We gave her a Bible, which she began reading daily.

This did not seem like the same girl we had known in Bilibid Prison tormented by devils, with her face distorted, screaming at the top of her voice. This was a perfectly normal Filipina girl who had recovered from the nightmare of demon possession.

I went through Clarita's court proceedings along with our church's lawyer, Pedro Jacinto, and petitioned for her release from Welfareville. When parole was granted, we placed her in the home of one of our best Christian families, the Sadorras. At that time, Mr. Sadorra was an intern and is now a medical doctor.

While living in Manila, Clarita became very unhappy because every time she appeared in public, people wanted to see her and talk to her. One day she left and went to the north of Luzon to live in a small town where she married a young rice farmer.

The last time I saw her, she had two children.

I asked her husband, "What kind of wife do you have?"

"Oh, a good woman."

I asked, "Is she crazy?"

"Oh, no."

"Does she ever go mad or say that the spirits bite her?" I asked.

"No, but she told me that she was in jail, and a white man came. That's you. You broke that spell over her, and she has been free ever since."

At last report, she is living a simple life and is active with a local congregation.

The victory was sure. Christ again proved himself to be the answer!

But that was not the end of the miracle.

A detailed account of Clarita's deliverance was printed in *The Philippines Free Press* and all the other papers and broadcast widely by all the radio stations. The news accounts were filled with the testimony of God's power. The Lord wonderfully used all the publicity.

Suddenly, I was a celebrity. Our work instantly became known all over the Philippines. With my picture on the front page of newspapers and in magazine articles, people would recognize me wherever I went. It gave me recognition that otherwise would have taken many years to receive.

When I walked down the streets, twenty people would suddenly fall down on their knees and kiss my fingers before I could stop them.

One time I entered the post office to buy a sheet of stamps, and the clerk behind the window said, "There's Doctor Sumrall. He casts out devils." Everybody in the line fell on their faces and knees. Embarrassed, I walked toward the counter — I was now the only one standing — while they grabbed at my hand to kiss it.

The mayor proved to be a real friend. Suddenly, we had total official cooperation, sometimes getting permits and inspections okayed on the same day we asked for approval — and without ever paying any bribes.

When it came time to pay for our final building permit, our new friend, the mayor, passed a special city ordinance to give it to us free — something that the newspapers lauded. The special ordinance required the consent of all the members of the official board of the Manila City Council, but after all the publicity, not one of them spoke against us.

Bethel Temple was the first Protestant church in the city to receive a free building permit. This act of kindness saved us what then was a great deal of money.

As he handed the permit to me, the mayor said, "You're the first Protestant that ever got anything free in this city. Is there anything else you want?"

I said, "Yes, there is."

"What is it?" he asked.

"I would like to preach in Roxas Park, called the Sunken Gardens, across the street," I replied.

This beautiful spot in Intramuros Spanish City is a place for special gatherings. It is the most centrally located spot in the nation.

"For how long?" asked the mayor.

"Oh, about six weeks," I replied.

"Six weeks! That's a long time. How long does it take for you tell your story?"

"Well, it will take a long time to say all I've got to say."

"The girl is healed," he said abruptly, "you can have the park as long as you want it," and he wrote down a permit for me to use the city park across from city hall.

While we were preparing for our revival meetings, Gordon Lindsay in Texas — who did not know our plans — sent us thousands of magazines with testimonies in them. Also without knowing about the upcoming crusade, Oral Roberts sent me a film on healing, complete with projector, a screen, and everything to go with it.

Through Ruben Candelaria, superintendent of the Methodist church in the Manila area, God miraculously opened up the Methodist churches of the city to us for services. I went to all of them, preaching, showing the film, and distributing the magazines. By the time we held the park meetings, the whole city was aflame.

One night when I preached, over five thousand men came up to receive the Lord as their Saviour. With their wives, that meant ten thousand. With their children it became over twenty thousand. That's almost the population of an entire city saved in one night!

With the preaching of evangelist Clifton Erickson, we saw the crowds grow to sixty thousand a night.

During the six weeks of revival meetings, one hundred and fifty thousand people made a profession of their faith and filled out cards, indicating their commitment to Christ. We had boxes and boxes of cards.

Some of those saved were from the highest ranks of society.

The most popular movie actor in the whole country, Carlos Padilla, received a miracle. He could walk again, by the power of God. The people went almost insane with joy when they saw this movie idol healed by God's mighty power.

A crippled lawyer who worked in the courthouse in downtown Manila had walked on two crutches for twelve years. Everybody knew him. One night during our revival, he was healed.

When he walked into the city hall the next day without his crutches, people said, "You must be his brother. You can't be the cripple."

He replied, "No, I'm him. I've been healed by the mighty power of God."

Every kind of miracle imaginable was witnessed.

The Taytay Methodist Church paid for a fifteen minute radio program to be broadcast on a powerful station that covered the whole nation. Every night, right after the news, I talked about what was happening in the Manila crusades. Over the radio, I told what God was doing for others and invited people to come and see for themselves.

As a result, people traveled from all over the country to attend the meetings. Not one city was unrepresented.

In the Philippines today, there are several million people who were saved because of that great deliverance of that one girl. God can do more in one minute than we can do in fifty years. Satan's power was broken, and the people were set free. It was a glorious and exciting moment in our lives.

Oral Roberts put the story in his magazine and called it "The Miracle That Changed a Nation."

It was true. The crusade held in Roxas Park fired the greatest revival the city — or the nation — had ever experienced. Throughout the Philippines, even once-empty, dead churches became alive with people searching for God.

During this time, we were also able to complete the church building in downtown Manila. In fact, 75 percent of the money to build the temple came from the local people. Most of them were poor, but with fifty thousand people giving at one time, the offerings multiplied quickly.

It would take six or eight people from eight in the morning until three in the afternoon just to count the money collected from the previous evening's service. Then we would give it to the contractor, and he'd keep building. Eventually, the church was completed — debt-free.

When we started the great crusade in the Philippines, the newspapers wanted to print stories criticizing our ministry. The Go Puan Seng family, however, who owned one of Manila's newspapers, came to our defense.

Earlier God had led me to their home to pray for their demon possessed daughter. Although she had lost her mind completely, God had healed her instantly when I laid hands on her.

Because of my friendship with them, the Go family told the press, "Don't write those lies. This is a good man. He healed a member of our family."

Mrs. Go, who was a leader in the community, had many wealthy Chinese friends. If one of them was ill, she would have her chauffeur pick me up and take me to their home to pray for them.

Then Mrs. Go would call them and say, "Why don't you give his church an offering?"

I'd come back home with enough money to keep our building contractor working for a week. Many of her friends made donations to the building.

The Go family came to our aid again when a group of doctors claimed we were healing people without a permit. These physicians went so far as to bring charges against us in court.

When I arrived at the courthouse to defend myself, I found two judges and three lawyers who had come to defend *me*.

One of the judges, who held a higher position than the judge hearing the case, told the presiding judge, "We go to this man's meetings every night. People are getting blessed and healed. This is the best thing that ever came to the Philippines."

Without hesitating, the judge said, "Case dismissed."

We continuously marveled at how God gave us favor in the eyes of those in authority.

Even President Magsaysay, who was then leader of the Philippine government, took a very special interest in our church.

When Oral Roberts came over to visit, I took him in to see the president and he told Roberts, "In this country Christ is the answer, and we all know it."

That was the name of my church, Bethel Temple — Christ is the Answer Church.

The president had decided that my church was the answer to all the problems in the Philippines. And he was right.

This congregation of believers continues to have a positive effect on the Philippines, which has suffered greatly in recent years because of political corruption. Many Christians are fighting for good within the Philippine government.

Today, Bethel Temple is the largest worship center in the country, and the people still crowd in. The revival didn't stop; it is still going on.

My great-nephew, David Sumrall, pastors Bethel Temple, attended by almost nineteen thousand people on Sundays. He is in the process of building a new glass building that will seat around ten thousand when completed. His church has special outreaches for the professional young people, meetings for college graduates, and the largest Bible school in the country.

Since Manila has so many people from the outlying provinces, Bethel Temple has multiple services every Sunday. People come according to their province of origin.

Services begin at seven o'clock in the morning with singing and preaching in the dialect of that particular province, say Ilocano. Then at eight o'clock, we have a service in one of the other dialects, such as Pampango. The nine o'clock service may be in Tagalog, which is the native language around Manila— and so it goes all day.

It is amazing that after twenty-five years, the revival and its effects are still apparent. Many new, evangelistic churches have risen throughout Manila, which has a population of more than two million.

Native Christian leaders have been trained and now do evangelistic work throughout this country of about 66 million people. My dream to build a great evangelistic center to help evangelize the Philippines became a reality.

20
Running With the Vision

One day I unknowingly walked into the middle of an anti-American protest in downtown Manila. One sign said "Go home white monkeys." Another read "America is imperialist."

Shocked by such a display of hatred and disrespect, I went over to the boy who was carrying a sign.

"Son," I asked, "am I a monkey?"

"I don't think so," he answered.

"That's what your sign says."

"It does?" he said. "I hadn't looked at it."

"Then, what are you doing with it?"

"Oh," he told me, "I was standing over on that corner, and a man gave me some money to come out here and hold this sign."

"Well," I told him, "seeing that you don't believe that, throw it down."

He did and even stomped on it.

I walked over to another boy. "Now, son, you're a historian, aren't you?"

He said, "No, I'm really not."

"Oh, your sign says that America is imperialist. You

- 199 -

must know something about American history at least as it relates to the Philippines."

"No, I don't really know anything."

"Well, what are you doing with that sign?"

"Well," he answered, "a man gave me some money and told me to carry it in front of the Congress building."

By this time I was so angry. I prayed, "God, this makes me so upset. I give my life to these people, and then they say such crazy things against my country."

The Lord said, "That's what I wanted you to see. America is in even worse shape than the Philippines. You need to go home and help save your own country. You can still travel overseas, but you need to have your foundation and your footings in America."

"I don't want to go home," I protested. "I like it here. This is home to me."

"No," answered the Lord. "I want you to go home to America. Preach hard and help save America."

Then the Lord began to tell me what would happen in America. He said that university students would riot and burn the buildings.

Sex and homosexuality would be flaunted in the news and entertainment media. His laws would be disdained and His people mocked.

He told me that the scourge of paganism and spiritualism was going to come to America. Foreign religions would be believed by people living on our own block and in our own community. I couldn't believe it.

I said, "No, no! I've been to heathen lands. They don't have anything to offer our people."

God said, "Americans will accept false teaching, and they will be hurt by it. They'll go to hell because they believe the lies of the devil."

In the past several years, I've watched these things come to pass, exactly as the Lord showed me.

"God," I asked, "how can I help America?"

"You will never help America unless you can get My

message to the people," He told me. "You won't be heard if you don't go on television."

I didn't know much about television, but I had done a few shows. "I'll develop a program for television."

God said, "No, I'm not talking about that. Your ministry must own stations. A network of Christian stations will be the channel of truth to America. You must do it."

You know, at that time I was living in Manila. Very few Americans had ever heard of me.

"How can a little guy help save America?" I asked. "I don't see how it can happen."

"I'll give you TV stations," the Lord answered. "You will speak to millions of people."

I went upstairs and told my wife, "Honey, we're going to go back to America. I'm going to appoint another pastor for the church here in Manila. The Lord said He needed me more in America than in the Philippines."

That word from the Lord was confirmed when a cable arrived from America. The pastor I had left at Calvary Temple in South Bend had left the church. The congregation appealed to us to return home.

Just to make sure it was time for us to leave Manila, I asked the Lord once again, "Why must we go?"

He said, "If you stay here, they will worship you and not Me."

I knew God was right, as usual. I had done my job, and it was time to go home.

With more sorrow than I can measure, with more tears than I can record, my wife and I and our sons prepared to return to the States. Now we had three sons, with Peter having been born in Manila on October 17, 1953.

Thousands came to the airport to see us off. After we boarded our flight, the people cried so loud that the control tower recalled our plane from the runway.

The captain said to me, "Can you go down and do

something with those people? The tower won't let me take off with them screaming and crying for you."

I went back and, consoling them again, promised I would be back every year.

I have kept that promise and returned regularly to Manila.

When I arrived back in this country with my wife and children, I owned only a modest house and ten acres in South Bend. The Lord told me that He had given us that property for my new work.

Others, however, thought I should quit.

One pastor told me bluntly, "Sumrall, you're over fifty, and you're finished."

"That's not true," I said.

But I went inside and prayed, "God, did you hear that preacher?"

He answered, "Yes."

"Is what he said true?"

"No," the Lord told me. "You've got to run with the vision. You're just getting started in your ministry."

Once again, I obeyed.

We wrote all the friends we had in America and explained, "We are going to begin building our offices for a world ministry, and we'd like you to help us."

They sent in a little money and construction began.

I had never done any business with South Bend's American National Bank, but they sent their first vice president over just as the steel walls went up, giving us just a skeleton of a building.

"I'm looking for Sumrall," he said to me.

"I'm Lester Sumrall," I replied, shaking his hand.

"I'm with American National Bank," he said. "Do you have a loan on this building yet?"

"No, sir," I said. No one would lend me money since I had just gotten back from overseas.

"We'll make a loan to you," he said, "if you'll come to our offices and receive it."

"Would you loan me enough?" I asked.

"We'll loan you what you need. Do you know how much you need?"

"Yes. To put on the roof and get the building ready for us to move in and start using it, I need $140,000."

"We'll loan you that amount."

Once again God had given us favor with those in a position to help us.

When the building was finished, I said to myself, "I better start with radio, that's cheaper than television."

I guess I really didn't have enough faith at that time to believe God for a television station. Instead, I petitioned the Federal Communications Commission, and they gave me a radio channel, FM 103.9, and we went on the air.

Since my ministry now owned a radio station, we joined the National Religious Broadcasters Association. When I went to their national convention in Washington, DC, I met a man who said, "Congratulations on your radio station. But what you need is television."

God said, "Yes."

I said to myself, *I don't have any money. How am I going to get a TV station?*

The man said, "I have one I will sell you for a million dollars. It's worth several million. Sign here."

"Do it," confirmed the Lord.

I went ahead and signed the contract to purchase the station.

The seller and I both petitioned the FCC to change the ownership over to LeSea Broadcasting (Lester Sumrall Evangelistic Association).

Two or three weeks later, I received a letter from a doctor in Oregon along with a $94,000 check.

"Hey, God," I prayed, "this is a little unusual."

"Well," he said, "having a TV station is unusual, too."

A few weeks after that, a medical doctor in Anderson, Indiana, gave me $65,000 — and other money began to come in.

When the FCC said LeSea could have the station, we were ready to complete the transaction. I had just enough, to the dollar, to pay for it.

Today I personally minister to over four million Americans over the television stations the Lord has provided. Our ten-station network reaches such cities as Grand Rapids, Oklahoma City, South Bend, Tulsa, Honolulu, Indianapolis, and Denver. We're also on cable and two satellite systems, giving us access to almost all of the United States. Almost every day a new channel of ministry opens to us.

God did just as He told me He would before I left the Philippines.

On the property the Lord gave us, we built our Bible school university.

Today, we also have a beautiful church, a big domed building that seats thousands. It is the largest church in our entire area.

How did we do it?

We obeyed— and the Lord did great things.

After we returned to South Bend and got established in our ministry, the Lord sent us to Hong Kong.

It didn't take us long to discover that the Chinese were quite different from the Filipinos. That took some adjustment on my part.

Our first crusade was held in the South China Football Stadium, which seats about one hundred thousand. Unlike the Filipino crowds, only about five thousand attended. That was just enough, however, to seat everyone in the executive section of the stadium — the air-conditioned sky-box where the wealthy sit to watch sports events.

At the end of two weeks of meetings in the football stadium, I baptized 300 people who then became the nucleus of our first church. All we needed now was a building in which to hold services.

In Hong Kong land is sold by the square inch and

even a small lot can cost millions of dollars. I knew we couldn't build a new church, so I suggested we look for a meeting hall.

When I approached the agent who was selling space in the tallest building in Hong Kong at that time, he said, "All the floors in this building are sold, but an athletic group who owns one floor has been bickering among themselves. They now want to sell. The property hasn't gone on the market yet. But once it does, the space will go quickly."

Once again, the Lord supplied the money for us, and we purchased the entire fourth floor of this huge building located in the heart of the city. That became the mother church.

When it was time to start other churches in Hong Kong, the Lord showed us an interesting way to obtain space.

The Chinese are very status conscious and consider the ground floor of a building undesirable. In many high rise apartment buildings, the ground floor was difficult to sell because nobody wanted to live there.

Whenever possible, we would purchase two or three apartments on the ground floor of a building and turn them into a church. This worked to our advantage because the people working on the upper floors had to pass by the church on their way to the street. It was perfect, and we marveled at how the Lord provided.

God gave us a sovereign work in Hong Kong that was of His will and His power. The tremendous fruit born among the believers there continues even today. In fact, I believe those churches will play an important role in evangelism when Communist China opens up to the gospel.

When will that be? That's what I wanted to know.

Not long ago, I was praying and asked, "Lord, how about China?"

God told me "The Communist regime in China will

fall as Russia's did. The Chinese got their doctrine from Russia, and they will fall like Russia did. They will fall on their face from hunger. Then the doors to the country will swing open. Those preachers in the underground will become upper ground, and there will be the greatest revival that history has ever known."

That's what God wants in these last days. He doesn't want peanuts. He wants us to save entire nations. China has more people than any other country on the face of the earth — one billion, five hundred million.

"How do we reach them?" I asked.

The Lord told me, "They won't follow you unless they hear you."

The government broadcasts to its people by short-wave, and most Chinese homes have a short-wave radio. Recently, our ministry asked the American government to give us a permit for a short-wave station so we could broadcast into China.

They gave us a permit for 12.5 million watts, which is very powerful.

This station will be in the middle of the Pacific Ocean and can reach three billion human beings. When listeners hear the broadcasts in Shanghai, it will sound as if we were in the suburbs. We will come in so strong that the weaker stations will be drowned out.

When this project is completed with our three short-wave radio stations, we will be speaking with the strongest voice on the face of the earth.

The Lord also told me, "When China is ready, have a large boat in every port and harbor in China, with a million dollars worth of rice on board. Then tell the Chinese people that Jesus loves you and He's alive — come and dine!"

Hallelujah!

These are not mere dreams. We've already made deposits on the equipment needed to obey the Lord.

Although our ministry is based in South Bend, Indiana, I have continued to minister around the world, just as the Lord had promised. Preaching God's Word has continued to be my top priority.

Once, when I arrived at the Caracas airport in Venezuela, early on a Sunday morning, no one was there to meet me.

After waiting for quite a while, I became very discouraged. *Here I've come to preach and these missionaries have forgotten all about me,* I thought.

My Spanish was so basic that I couldn't set off on my own to find them. Carrying my suitcase, I walked outside and waved down a taxi. Somehow I explained to the driver that I wanted to go to an evangelistic church — any evangelistic church.

Thirty minutes later we stopped at a Baptist church.

It was too early for services to begin, so I just looked around, trying to figure out what to do.

Noticing a doorbell, I rang it. Out came a young American.

"Sir, I'm sorry but I'm lost," I said. "The missionary didn't meet me at the airport. I don't know where to go. I told the taxi driver to bring me to an evangelistic church, and I hope I'm not imposing on you. My name is Lester Sumrall."

"I don't believe it," he said. "Are you the real Lester Sumrall?"

"What's wrong?"

"Nothing is wrong. A miracle has taken place."

"Well," I said, "what's so miraculous about being stuck at a foreign airport?"

"Oh, that had to be God."

"What do you mean?"

"I have a book you wrote and was just now reading it upstairs," he said. "I was sitting there, and I said, 'God, is this man still living?' and God said, 'Yes.' I asked, 'God, is it possible that you could bring this man to my door?' "

That Baptist preacher grabbed me and gave me a

great big hug.

I preached in his church that morning.

Just as I was ending my sermon, the missionary who should have picked me up at the airport poked his head in the back door.

"Well, hello," I greeted him. "Why did you leave me stranded in an airport?"

He was very apologetic. "I live fifty miles away from here. I was going to have you at my place in time for church this morning, but I had a blow-out on the road. I couldn't get anybody to help me.

"While waiting, I prayed, 'Lord, Lester Sumrall is over there in the airport, and I've got a blow-out on the road. I don't know what to do.' But the Lord assured me that everything was under control."

I had to chuckle. "Well," I said, "that's the first time I have ever known of God blowing out a tire to answer prayer."

God is good.

He has been faithful in the little things and in the big ones.

While preaching in Tokyo, Japan, I received an urgent telephone call. Wherever I am in the world, my family and staff always know when and where to find me.

"Your mother passed away thirty minutes ago," I was told.

I said, "I'll be right home."

When I told my hosts my mother had died, they offered to drive me to the airport.

I quickly packed and caught a midnight plane out of Japan.

On the way home, I began to regret not being there when she went to be with the Lord. Then I realized that I had been doing exactly what she had told the Lord she wanted me to do — preaching in a pagan land.

God had honored my mother's prayers.

A few years later, I was in Singapore at the beginning

of a tour of the Orient. Just as I had done years before with Brother Carter, I was working my way up toward the Philippines, Hong Kong, and Japan with meetings scheduled all along the way.

While preaching, I was called to the phone and told my sister Leona had died. I immediately caught a plane home and preached her funeral.

Her death was a great personal loss to me. In her eyes, I could do no wrong, and to me she was my beloved little sister. We were very close. I loved her almost more than anybody else in the whole world, and I knew I had held a special place in her heart, too.

During these times of sorrow, God was faithful as always. It blessed me to know my dear mother and sister were being received into heaven with the welcome words, "Well done, good and faithful servant."

21

Teamwork

O ne Sunday night, after preaching in Stockholm, Sweden, I boarded a nonstop flight to Chicago. For the first few moments, I sat back in my seat, quietly rejoicing over the many people who had received Christ as their Saviour that evening at the meeting.

When I arrived in Chicago, where I was to take another plane to Florida, to my surprise, my wife and my son Stephen met me — their faces grim.

I knew it must be something serious for them to travel from South Bend to Chicago.

My wife said, "Stephen has something to tell you."

He was nervous. "I don't know how . . . ."

"Go ahead and say it," I said.

"We don't have the TV station in South Bend anymore," he said. "Yesterday it burned to the ground. The newspapers said it was a $12 million loss. It is the worst thing that we've ever known in our whole ministry. There was nobody in the building except the engineer who was putting taped programs on the air."

"How did it happen?" I asked.

"It was caused by an electrical surge from the power

company," Stephen explained. "Our wires couldn't take it and burst into flames."

"You have to go see what happened," said Stephen.

"No, I don't go see fires," I said. "I'm supposed to go to Florida and preach tonight."

"But we don't have a TV station."

"Well, there's nothing I can do about it today."

"You mean you're not going to go see it?"

"No."

I went to Florida and preached that night.

I'm sure people were saying, "Can you imagine a man going and preaching in another city when the embers are still hot from the fire that destroyed his ministry's flagship TV station?"

Being faithful to God is more important to me than a TV station. I had promised, and fifteen hundred people were expecting me. So I went.

When I returned to South Bend, my son Peter said, "Daddy, it was a sad day, but it was also a very glorious day. The city had never seen such a raging fire. While I was watching, the managers of the local commercial stations showed up."

In South Bend, we have three network stations and our ministry's station.

All three offered, "Peter, what can we do?"

"I was so frustrated," he told me, "that I said, 'Get me on the air.' "

God once again gave us favor, and these men said, "We'll do it. Where?"

"Over at the church," Peter said. "We've got all kinds of room."

By 6 p.m. our station was back on the air.

The commercial stations gave us expensive equipment to use and told us, "Don't bother to bring it back — this is a gift to you."

On the front page, the newspapers printed a large picture of the fire accompanied by a very sympathetic article. For the first time since our ministry began, the people of South Bend looked with favor toward our operation.

God took a tragedy and turned it into a blessing for our ministry.

The fire also had another positive effect.

I saw my sons take charge in my absence and handle a difficult situation with great maturity.

My goal had always been to build a team ministry with my three sons. To do that, I knew I had to give away some of my control and authority. I couldn't hold onto the reins and make every decision.

As the administrator of our ministry, Stephen manages the personnel, signs all the checks, and pays the bills. When documents come in of a legal nature, I have Stephen check them over. Whenever I am out of the country, I know the ministry is in good hands.

My youngest son, Peter, is vice president and chief operations manager of all the TV and radio stations. His expertise in that area is a gift, and knowing he's in charge lifts a tremendous burden from my shoulders.

Frank, the oldest of my sons, co-pastors the church in South Bend with me. Our congregation loves him — he's full of joy and has the gift of evangelism. His pastor's heart often leads him to seek out the lost or to pray with those who are in need of comfort or healing.

Frank and my second son, Stephen, are both excellent preachers of the gospel. Often, when I'm listening to a tape of one of their sermons, something they say will jolt me into a new realization of God's goodness or will send me searching God's Word.

Where did they get that from, I wondered, *and why didn't I see it first?*

Today many young people, who rise like a rocket in ministry, come down very early in life and are never able to reach the same height of blessing, anointing, or achievement again.

My sons have avoided that experience because the Lord trained them on the job just as He had done with me. I think that's why all three of my sons have been able to find their callings within our family ministry.

When they were participating in Manila, Hong Kong, and all the other places that they accompanied me, God was preparing them. By including them in every phase of the ministry, my sons knew they weren't just tagging along. Even at the age of twelve and fifteen they were competent and responsible — no one ever called them greenhorns.

From the beginning, my sons knew our ministry was their ministry, too. That's why today I can call on them to make important decisions.

Sure, there are times when one of them has made a poor judgment call, but I just lean back and ask myself, *Let me see, he is 36 years old. When I was 36, what kind of decisions did I make?* Then, I smile and say to my son, "Son, you made a good decision."

If we judge people from our own age and experience, we'll come to the wrong conclusion about them every time.

I believe that in this last generation, God is going to use youth as well as maturity to assist in performing the greatest revival earth has ever known. But it's going to take teamwork.

Men of God are not permitted to be selfish. Selfishness ruins a team the same way it ruins any marriage.

Sometimes when I counsel with married couples, I hear them say, "I'm not treated right. I'm not given my part. I've done everything I can — it's time that my spouse wakes up to the fact that I . . . ."

That's when I interrupt them and say, "You are full of the devil. Read Isaiah and you will see how many times the devil says 'I.' You have to get 'I' out of your conversation and your thoughts and put 'you' in. You have to start loving the other person. If you give 52 percent, and your marriage partner gives 52 percent, then you have four percent left over for the neighbors."

Selfishness destroys; it never builds.

One day the general superintendent of one of America's largest denominations went to a conference in Wales and died of a heart attack. I had been writing his biography for a couple of years. He would come and stay at our home in South Bend for a day or two, and we would work on his life story. The book was just about finished when he died.

I thought, *Oh, there goes two years of work down the drain. What in the world am I going to do?*

I asked his wife, "Ruth, would you come to South Bend so we can finish this biography. You can stay with a family from our church."

She agreed.

My dear friend, Dr. Howard Carter, was visiting in our home at the time, so in the evenings I'd say, "Phone Ruth and invite her to come over and eat dinner with us."

Sometimes, my wife fed the boys separately so that the adults could talk freely without interruption. I would sit at the head of the table with Louise by my side while Ruth and Brother Carter sat on the other side of the table together.

After dinner, Howard would say, in his best English accent, "May I help you to your motor car?"

This went on for several evenings. Sometimes, it took him half an hour just to take her fifty steps into the yard.

One day, he asked, "Mr. Sumrall, would you talk to me?"

I said, "Sure.

He said, "What do you think if I marry Ruth?"

"She's pretty and certainly very intelligent," I said. She was about fifty, and he was into his early sixties. "It seems to me that it would be all right."

"Would you be my best man and stand up beside me?" he asked.

I said I would be proud to do that.

So they got married and were very happy together. But, like any couple, they occasionally had their differences.

One day Brother Carter came to my house and said, "Mr. Sumrall, don't ever marry a widow."

"Why not?"

"You see," he said in his wry, British way, "the greatest man that ever lived, died."

I chuckled.

They lived in Springfield, Missouri, for a while, then went back to England and taught in the Bible school, both of them, for a year or two. After that, they went to New Zealand and pastored a church.

They were married for over twenty-five years.

Howard Carter lived to be eighty-seven and preached until the day that he died. He was a great, great man.

Today if you visit the churches that he and I founded in Europe or Java, you might say, "How in the world did you two pay for all this?"

We didn't. We listened to the Lord and obeyed. Then He provided the finances.

Obedience is so important. Howard Carter's miracle-filled life is an example of that.

God is not a tyrant who stands over us with a club. In order to enjoy His perfect will and live in His wonderful plan for our lives, however, we must listen carefully and obey.

Although I am well into what most people consider their retirement years, I still have to listen and obey. As a result, the blessings continue.

I have ministered in 110 nations, and I travel constantly even today. Yet, I am still required to obey Him. Although I might be tempted to sit back on my laurels and admire all that God has permitted me to do, I must still listen to His voice.

If there is any one thing that I hope you are learning

from this book, it is that we must obey God.

To do that effectively, we have to get into the Word. **Daily** Bible reading must be the bare minimum. Start there and work up to spending hours studying the Word every day.

You'll only understand the Bible if you connect with its author. I encourage you to spend quality time with the Lord daily. After all, how can you obey someone whose voice you do not know?

In this final hour of the Church, God wants people who will obey Him. He wants to set the world free from all the devices the devil has sent to destroy mankind. To do that, He needs both the young — and the old.

Remember, in his final forty years, Moses performed more miracles through the Spirit of God than any other person in the Bible.

Jesus performed thirty-six recorded miracles. Moses did about forty-four.

When this eighty-year-old prince-turned-nomad walked across the sands of the Sinai into Egypt, he was austere and bold, walking tall, casting a long shadow. You couldn't miss him when you saw him coming. With his chin tilted, you had to give heed to what he said. His fierce eyes were penetrating.

"God willing, I'll set you free," he told the Israelites and led his people out of bondage and death.

Moses' story teaches us that your age has nothing to do with what God can do. The greatest period of Moses' ministry began when he was eighty years old. In fact, the Lord did not let Moses retire until he was 120 years old — and then God took him immediately.

Only you can decide when it is time for you to be discarded.

I have prepared for my death by making sure that nothing will happen to adversely affect our ministry. I don't have any real estate, financial accounts, or anything. When I die, the ministry will just carry right on.

I don't believe, however, I will be called to heaven any time soon. In fact, I hope to be a very old preacher, participating in this next great revival that God has in mind.

There are a lot of things that I have not accomplished — not yet.

22

The Jerusalem Vision

Not long ago, I was sitting in a church service in Panama City, Florida, praying and preparing my heart to preach. Suddenly, I saw a river of blood.

It was the most amazing thing you could ever imagine. I couldn't even see the sides of the river, it was so wide.

There was no place of origin, but it was flowing toward me — thick, crimson blood.

When I got up to preach, I told the congregation, "I haven't seen a vision in years, but I saw a river of blood here tonight, just as clear as I can see you with my eyes. My spiritual eyes saw a river of blood flowing toward me."

The next night I was preaching in Birmingham, Alabama. While I was sitting in the front pew waiting to go up on the platform, the river of blood came back.

I blinked my eyes, trying to make it go away.

I thought, *Boy, there it is again. I sure hope that this doesn't happen the rest of my life.*

I didn't know what it was. I thought that it might be some kind of judgment.

This time I got upset and told the people, "This is the second night that I have seen this. Will you write it down in your Bible — and the date, please." They did.

I came home to South Bend and spoke to several men who are elders of our church. "I saw a river of blood. I saw it two nights. It might be judgment. Would you seek the Lord and ask Him what this is all about?"

Two or three days later, one of those brothers came to me. While he was praying, the Lord told him what the river of blood was.

It was not what we thought at all.

Remember when Noah came out of the ark, God said, "You can eat the vegetables and the fruit. You can eat the fish in the sea and the animal meat — but you cannot eat blood. The life of the flesh is in the blood."

This brother said to me, "The Lord said that what you saw was a river of life. The Lord is going to pour life into you and your ministry. It is going to be so wide that you can't see the ends of it over here on the sides. It is going to be so fantastic you won't be able to tell where it started from."

I said, "Really?"

"That's what the Lord said. There will be times when you won't even be able to count what God is doing. He will be doing it so great and fast that you won't have any control over it."

The next week I was in Denver talking to pastors about our ministry's new station that would soon be going on the air. Forty or fifty preachers attended, and as they started to leave, one came up to me and said, "You know, I came here especially because the Lord says that He has a message for you."

"What do you mean?" I asked rather coldly.

I don't like anybody prophesying over me. If God has something to say to me, I've got ears to hear. There are too many people running around telling other people what God said, when God hasn't said anything. Most of the stuff that people prophesy doesn't ever come to pass. So I didn't give him a very good reception.

He began to cry.

"Don't cry," I said.

"I don't know what the Lord is going to say, but the Lord is going to say something to you," he told me.

"Well," I said, "go ahead."

He closed his eyes and told me, "Your life is like a tree planted in God. Your life is a tree, and there are branches on your tree. Your first evangelism as a young man is a branch on your tree. That tree has so many branches upon it. Your missionary branches bore much fruit and still do. Your church is a branch. There are so many branches. Your television ministry is a branch. Your radio ministry is a branch." He mentioned things that he couldn't have known unless God had told him.

He suddenly stopped and looked at me.

After a short pause he said, "Thus saith the Lord, a new branch will spring forth upon your tree of life. It will be larger than all of the other branches. It will bear so much fruit that you will be amazed." Then he walked out the door.

"God," I prayed, "don't you know that I'm an old man now. I don't need any more branches."

"You are just about old enough for Me to trust you," God answered.

Some men God has trusted have taken His money and built themselves empires. Some got into trouble and couldn't pay for it. God never intended for that to happen. Preachers don't get into financial trouble by winning souls. They get into financial difficulty building empires.

Now I had two rivers of blood and one tree.

I said, "Lord, I'm afraid of it."

A couple of weeks later we went to the Holy Land with a group of 528 people. When we arrived at the Sea of Galilee, we all wanted to cross it together, so our five big boats were tied together.

It was such a brilliant day, and we could see all over the whole area — almost from shore to shore. I would point out where Jesus' miracles took place, and everyone would shout. People in nearby boats wondered what was happening, as we sang and praised God in the middle of the sea that Jesus so loved. I will never forget it as long as I live. We were all touched.

That night in Jerusalem, I went to bed about eleven o'clock. At ten minutes to midnight I was awakened by the Lord. He said, "I want to talk to you."

I got up, went into the next room, turned on the light, and got my pencil ready.

He said, "It is also midnight in prophetic time."

That shook me clear to my feet.

The Lord said, "I want you to listen to Me."

Believe me, He had my attention.

Then He said the strangest thing. "One of My greatest concerns is My own people, part of My church. I don't want them to suffer death by starvation before I return. Will you feed My people?"

I wanted to say "No," so loud that He could hear it. I don't know anything about feeding anybody. I'm a preacher, not a fry cook. I had no intention of feeding anybody. But I listened carefully.

"To them it will be an angelic food supply. It will be a miracle to them."

I sat there writing it all down from midnight until five o'clock in the morning.

"Hunger is an agonizing death," He said. "I want you to give to those who are dying. If you will, I will see that you live happily and victoriously. I will prosper you."

I had my heart set on building more television stations. I didn't answer Him back. I just sat there.

He said, "I have spoken to you in Jerusalem. It is the city where I took bread, blessed it, and broke it, saying, 'Take and eat. This is My body that is broken for you.' I want you to take the bread of the Spirit and the bread of the soul, and the bread of the body to the multitudes who are hungry on this earth."

I asked, "Just what do You mean?"

"Never take just bread. Never! Never! Don't merely feed people's bodies. Take bread to My church and give it to those who are hungry. In the last days, there is going to be famine such as this world has never seen."

He told me to call it the "End-time Joseph Program" and to acquire great amounts of food and housing in certain parts of the world so that when famine hits, we will be the ones who have food.

"You are to do this by telling pastors around the world that they should collect special offerings and give it to this mission. I will raise up ten thousand pastors around the world, and they will give to this ministry. You will take it and give it to pastors in starving nations who will give it to their own hungry people.

"In many instances, you will have to take this in quickly by plane. If you send it by sea it will take too long, and corrupt officials will steal it from you."

God spoke to me again and said, "Millions of My people who belong to Me get up in the morning and say, 'Our Father, which art in heaven, hallowed be thy name. Thy kingdom come, thy will be done, on earth as it is in heaven. Give us today our daily bread.' But when the evening comes, their bellies are empty."

He got my attention.

I began to feel their pain. What if your children were hungry and you said the Lord's Prayer in the morning — but put your children to bed at night crying because they had no food?

He also told me that He speaks to people about it, but they still don't want to give.

The Lord asked, "Will you feed my little children?"

"Yes," I answered.

"You will greatly rejoice," He said.

For five hours He told me the way to do it, how to do

it, and even who would do it.

I said, "Lord, I am willing to be an instrument. As old as I am, I need no honor from man. I need no prestige at all. As old as I am, I need no earthly goods of any kind. I can't take a thing of this earth with me. All I want to do is work for You until You come. I want to bless Your church and to bless those who are without."

My friends, I want you to hear this and judge it well. If it is of the Lord, then we must obey.

I hope that is the one thing you have learned from this book — that you and I must obey the Lord.

Please seek the Lord about this. Search your heart. Catch this vision, my friends.

In the years ahead of us there will be famine, and out of the plenty of American Christians there will flow blessings to the ends of the earth.

You say, "When is it going to start?"

Today Somalia is dying. World relief agencies are frustrated that nobody wants to hear about it anymore. Americans have already grown cold to the cries coming from Somalia and Ethiopia and other places in Western Africa.

Albania is desperate, too — and things are very bad in Russia.

There was one very odd detail about the vision I received in Jerusalem. I kept hearing the word "Hercules."

Hercules? What could that mean? The only Hercules I knew about was the muscle-bound false god of Greek mythology.

Why would the Lord give me the name of a pagan, false god?

After I came back from Jerusalem and explained the vision to my sons and the ministry staff, I remember talking about how important it was going to be to gain our own airlift capability.

In Somalia, their shaky government collapsed and

various warlords took over. These thugs command about as much respect as your average New York City street gang. Virtually all relief supplies were being hijacked by gunmen from various warring factions. That's why the United Nations and eventually the United States sent in armed troops — to make sure the food got off of the boats and into legitimate warehouses, then off to the disaster area.

In most Third World countries, bringing in relief supplies can be frustrating. It disappears off the wharf before missionaries can come get it. Even if it doesn't disappear, corrupt government officials create preposterous "import fees" that are nothing less than bribery. In many countries, the customs duties can equal the market value of the product. That means if you import a $10 sack of wheat, you have to buy it for $10 in the United States, then upon arriving in the Third World, pay another $10 for permission to bring it into the country.

This can be a problem if you are bringing in $100,000 worth of wheat. It just tears you up to pay the Lord's money to some thief in charge of the docks.

Another problem involved in relief work is getting the food and supplies to the intended user. The infrastructure to deliver the goods does not exist in many parts of the world.

I saw how essential it was that we have our own airlift capability. We needed to be able to fly food into local airports across the globe. As I was sharing this with my South Bend staff, I turned to our ministry's aviation man, Thorpe Mitchell, and asked him, "Now, what is a Hercules?"

This man, who was sent by God in 1984 to pilot our ministry airplane, looked at me strangely and asked, "Why do you ask?"

"Well," I told him, "because God keeps saying to me: 'Hercules, Hercules.' "

Thorpe looked incredulous. "That is very interesting," he mused aloud, "because that's the only aircraft in the whole world that will do what you're talking about. Hercules is the name for the Lockheed C-130, which is primarily a military aircraft. It has four turbo-prop engines and is easily loaded from the rear. It will fly several thousand miles on a tank of gas and can carry a significant payload into a primitive, unimproved location.

"No other airplane can do that. Other aircraft can carry more cargo, go further distance, do it faster, and sometimes do it cheaper, but no other aircraft can take it into the primitive areas you are describing."

After he explained this to me, I said, "Well, get me one."

I have heard him say that at that moment, Thorpe Mitchell knew this was what the Lord had prepared him to do. Throughout his life, he had been uniquely trained and positioned to be able to do just that — to get us a Hercules military transport plane, fly it, and take care of it.

23

In the Middle of Miracles

Thorpe Mitchell had spent most of the 1960s in the United States military airlift command, so he had been all around the world. During the 1970s, Thorpe had been full-time in the reserves as an air operations officer. Then in the early part of the 1980s, he worked as a squadron commander over some 400 people, maintaining twenty-six U.S. Air Force F-4 fighter jets.

After coming to work for us, Thorpe had remained in the reserves and been assigned to Wright-Patterson Air Force Base in the headquarters of the Air Force Logistics Command which manages all of the weapons systems in the Air Force inventory.

Wright-Patterson is the largest Air Force Base in the world with some thirty-three thousand employees. It is commanded by a four-star general, with three-star generals under him, two-star generals below them, and so forth. On many Air Force Bases, I am told, the highest rank you'll ever see is a full colonel — Mitchell's rank.

Down the hall from his assignment was the Lockheed C-130 Hercules program office. The supervisor was Thorpe's personal friend.

Right off the bat, Mitchell warned me that a brand-new C-130 would cost $30 million. That is an awesome amount of money — the annual budget of some counties. We were in no position to even talk about that kind of money. So, I suggested we find a used one.

Indeed, Mitchell's friend suggested we check into four planes parked at Lake City, Florida. A privately-owned maintenance facility down there had done extensive work on the planes for the Peruvian government — which had not paid its bill. So, the company had slapped a lien on the aircraft and was now selling them to get paid for their work.

Right about that time, I had to speak at a meeting in Miami, then another one in Little Rock, Arkansas. Mitchell told me that Lake City wasn't really that far out of our way.

"Let's go look at those airplanes," I suggested.

We flew into Lake City, and there they were parked wing tip to wing tip, looking brand new. The company was asking four million dollars each for the planes. That was still an enormous amount for a ministry to raise.

We began to pray again.

One of the aircraft really stood out among the four. It had a brand new floor, and somebody had even chromed the tie-down rings on the cargo hold. Mitchell said he had never seen a C-130 that was quite as immaculate as this one.

We found out it had been a show plane for the Missouri Air National Guard before it was sold to Peru. Used to display the maintenance skills of the organization, it had been given a lot of extra tender loving care and was an extra-specially good aircraft.

We hired some specialists to check the plane out and their reports were amazing: To a man, they all said this was the best Hercules they'd ever flown. It was more responsive, had a little more power, and seemed to be in better overall condition than the average Hercules they were accustomed to flying.

We set up a meeting with the Peruvian naval attaché in Washington and hammered out a price of $1.5 million — considerably below the $4 million that they were asking. It was also a lot less than the $30 million for a new Hercules straight off of the Lockheed production line.

Still, we had to ask the Lord to help us come up with $1.5 million. That was hurdle number one.

The next two hurdles also depended on divine intervention.

First, the United States Department of State had to approve the sale of any modern, in-use military aircraft. They were absolutely puzzled by our application. They were used to requests being submitted by foreign governments or forest firefighters who use C-130s to combat big blazes in the national forests.

But a Christian ministry? There was just no precedent.

We also had to get the approval of the Federal Aviation Administration, which regulates civilian air matters in the United States. They, too, didn't seem to know how to respond to an Indiana church wanting to buy a Hercules to feed the hungry.

Our first near-disappointment came from the State Department. We were tipped off that our application was going to be denied.

Fortunately, the Lord had planted a friend in the White House, a man who had the ear of the president of the United States. He took it from there and sent a letter over to the State Department on White House stationary saying the president would like to see the sale approved. That was about all it took.

Our attorney called back and told us, "I don't know what you did, but the State Department has suddenly changed its mind and is going to approve your request."

Meanwhile, God began sending in the money for the plane.

The Lord continued to move other mountains, too. We saved $75,000 in Florida state sales tax when the Peruvian government agreed to fly "their" aircraft to Indiana for delivery — where we are tax-exempt.

Then, we saved another large amount when a government official gave us a ferrying certificate that normally would have cost $50,000 — just to deliver our "Peruvian" plane from Florida to Indiana.

One day, in the middle of all these miracles, the Lord asked me where my faith was.

I had been praying, "Why haven't we gotten that airplane yet?"

The Lord said to me, "Well, where are you going to put it when you get it? Didn't I tell you to build a church in the Philippines before the congregation came in? You did, and then the congregation came. I want you to build a hangar here although you don't have an airplane yet."

I went to work.

The hangar cost us around $700,000 and is the largest hangar at the South Bend airport. For a few weeks, we were something of a laughingstock in South Bend for building a hangar for a plane nobody thought we would ever get.

Now I know how Noah felt.

You see, we had been told point-blank by the commander at Youngstown, Ohio, "You can't afford a airplane like that C-130."

When he said that, I didn't change my expression although I was boiling inside.

As we walked out of his office I said to myself, *If the devil can own them, God can own one.*

Another Air Force commander in Florida took us aside and said, "You ain't gonna get a C-130." We just had to smile and leave it in God's hands.

While we were still looking for a plane, my son Peter had called an airplane broker and told him that we wanted a military C-130 Hercules. He told Peter he was out of his mind.

The broker wasn't about to waste his time looking for a C-130 that the government certainly wouldn't let us have.

A while back, Peter stopped by the broker's office and dropped off a picture of our Hercules. With a little more faith, that broker could have made a nice commission — but that was another miracle. The way God did it, we didn't have to pay anybody a commission.

What an incredible day it was to see our C-130 in front of our hangar at the airport. My heart was filled with joy. Once again, I obeyed, and God provided.

I don't think there's any end to this vision. I pray that eventually we will have at least six C-130s.

After we got our first Hercules, the Lord led us to a successful businessman named Don Tipton.

Years ago, God had spoken to Tipton and told him to equip an ocean-going ship, but He didn't tell him why or what to do with it. Don had obeyed and acquired a fishing factory ship. Then, he enlisted a bunch of volunteers and over five years cleaned up the ship, made it seaworthy, and brought it down to San Pedro, California, in the Long Beach area, where he lives.

About the same time that we got permission to fly our C-130, Don was taking his ship down to Nicaragua with a load of cargo for some missionaries.

On our very first "shakedown" flight of the C-130, we flew a load of cargo to a missionary in Guatemala. It was a dirt landing strip up in the mountains at the Indian town of Quetzaltenango.

When we got there, we buzzed over and picked up some cargo from Don's ship and delivered it all around. He was so impressed that he announced, "You can use our ship as much as you want. We belong to you."

From that time on, we've had exclusive use of his ship.

When he said that, I told him, "Well, I want to take a load of supplies over to Latvia, and we have to get there by August."

Don said, "Oh, no way. You don't have any idea what goes into loading this thing. It takes literally months to load this ship, and it's still on its way back from Nicaragua."

But I kept after him, and sure enough, the ship docked in Latvia, the day Gorbachev was put under house arrest. For three days we couldn't contact the captain of the ship to find out what had happened to them. We didn't know if they had been hijacked, sunk, or imprisoned.

When the coup collapsed, we found out that our people were standing on the docks, handing out food.

That ship is seven decks deep and carries 5,000 tons of food, which is ten million pounds. As I write this, it's all loaded and in the next few days will disembark on its way to feed the small nation of Albania.

The prime minister of that country talked with me in his office recently and said, "If you will bring your ship, you will be saving our children."

I said, "All right. You try to get this nation straightened out and our ministry will take care of the children."

I can remember when I have wanted to bless a little town, and got on my knees to ask God to make it possible. Now we are taking nations for God.

As I write this, our C-130 Hercules is in Denmark and tomorrow night will be in Albania.

Right after the Desert Storm War, we flew supplies to the starving Kurds in Iraq for two months — hundreds of thousands of pounds of food. When we arrived, a thousand people a day were dying of dysentery. We took in water purifiers and a military field kitchen and began to feed them. Today, many, many Kurds are alive and praising God because of our C-130.

We actually had to fly into the Islamic Republic of Iran to make our deliveries. If you remember, it was Iran that took the entire American embassy hostage for 444 days with the Ayatollah's blessing.

On the way there, the C-130 developed engine trouble during a stop-over in Cyprus. It was a weekend, and the missionaries there had to make an emergency cash loan of tens of thousands of dollars to help us get a new engine.

That was a miracle in itself. Not very many missionaries would just happen to have tens of thousands of dollars on hand for an emergency loan. These were poor missionaries, but the Lord had caused them to have the cash just when we so desperately needed that loan.

We were glad to be able to continue on our mission of mercy to the Kurdish refugees.

Recently, we sent two thousand tons of rice to the Philippines, and the people are already eating it right now.

Many other places are waiting for us to send food.

We are ready to fly some men into Panama to find the Christians and to feed people in the churches who are hungry. As soon as we can get permission to fly into that battered country, we are willing to move.

How glad we are that Jesus is ready and willing.

I could fill up an entire book with the adventures we have had with our airplane and the ship. But the main point I want to get across is that when I was obedient, God made a way.

The last great branch on my tree of life will be to feed the hungry around the world. That is what I have been told to do, and I must obey.

24

Will You Obey?

Recently, the pastor of a small church told his people, "Listen, we want to help Brother Sumrall feed the hungry, and we are going to take up an offering for it. I have committed us to $1,000 a month or $12,000 for this year."

He passed the plates and got $14,000 the first day.

Then he took up the offering again for the expenses of his church, and it was more than his people had ever given.

God has a way of doing things if we will just let Him — if we will obey.

The first time I began talking about the vision I had received in Jerusalem, my sons were a little apprehensive.

One of them spoke up and said, "What are we going to do about putting a new TV station on the air if all you are going to do is go around and talk about the hungry?"

I said, "The night that God spoke, He also said that if I would do this, He would prosper all that I am doing."

God has many avenues of blessing. He doesn't have to bless in just one way.

We are believing God to care for all our ministry's

needs — building TV stations, plus feeding millions of hungry people. It is a large undertaking. It is bigger then all of us put together and multiplied by hundreds. It is that big.

Will you help me?

I've been frustrated somewhat by the magnitude of this mission. Usually, the average American will give for two or three months, but if something more exciting comes along, they waver and forget about their first commitment.

God is reaching out to us to do something incredible. I sent an order recently to Copenhagen, Denmark. We need more meat to give to Albania.

When we took food into Russia, I asked one company about meat and they said, "Yes. If you'll send me a check for $80,000, we'll give you meat." So I sent a check for $80,000 and they gave us $250,000 of the best Danish ham anybody has ever tasted. The Russians loved it.

On every flight, we've taken ten thousand pounds of meat along with the flour and the other supplies. But we can't continue if people don't catch the vision.

You say, "Well, why don't you talk to rich business-men?"

God told us not to.

Why don't we ask the large denominations?

They all have their own projects.

The Lord told me, "My little people who represent Gideon's victorious army of three hundred can save the world."

The Lord said, "Do you remember the story of the rich man and the beggar?"

I said, "Yes. You told it, and I preached it. I ought to know about it."

He said, "The rich man fared sumptuously every day." Thousands of people looked up to him as a glorified prince, but he had a problem. At his gate was a persistent little beggar named Lazarus.

The rich man's servants said, "Lazarus, the boss wants you to get out of here."

He said, "I'm not leaving. I want a piece of bread."

They said, "If we give you a piece of bread, you will be back tomorrow for more. We can't do that.

"Lazarus, he's told us to get rid of you, to kick you out. You've got to get out of this gate. When the princes and princesses come tonight and these big, beautiful gates open and the beautiful chariots come rolling in here with those lovely horses, he doesn't want to see you down there crying, 'Give me a crumb.'"

The rich man's servants may have killed Lazarus because soon after that he was in heaven. But the rich man died, too.

The Bible says the rich man lifted up his eyes in hell and looked across the way. He saw Abraham, and there was Lazarus — he'd made it to paradise.

The rich man pleaded, "Abraham, would you let Lazarus bring me a bottle of champagne, please?"

Well, actually, he had come down the ladder a long way. He said, "Would you let him dip his finger in water? My parched tongue needs a drop of water."

I said, "Yes, Jesus, I know that story."

He said, **"I want to inform you of something. America is that rich man, faring sumptuously every day. They are the best fed people in the history of mankind, and the Third World countries are Lazarus. The poor do not want your car or your home — all they want is a crumb."**

Now, my friend, as you consider the story of my life and my reluctant obedience and how the Lord has blessed me for it, I ask you to seek Him.

When the Lord spoke to me that night in Jerusalem, I understood His heart.

"Because of men's sins," God said, "in these last days millions will die from starvation, but I don't want even one of my Christians to die of hunger."

I couldn't understand why He wanted to use me,

then He explained, "You've preached in 110 nations, and you love all those people. I want to use you to feed them."

I believe that the wealthy church in America and churches around the world have been called on to ensure that Christians worldwide do not go without food. I also believe that great evangelism and revival will occur if we will show compassion and feed the starving.

The Lord showed me in detail that all over the face of this earth there are the beginnings of famine.

Will you catch this vision? This may be my last great labor.

Join me to save millions from death by starvation.

Will you help feed God's people in the difficult days that are just around the corner?

Will you feed Christian children who are asking God to "give us this day, our daily bread?"

What does the Lord say to you?

Will you obey?

If you would like to write Lester Sumrall, or if you would like more information on the Feed the Hungry program, write to:

LeSea, Inc.
P.O. Box 12
South Bend, IN 46624

Dr. Lester Sumrall is founder and chairman of a worldwide missionary outreach, The Lester Sumrall Evangelistic Association (LeSea). Respected throughout the world as a missionary statesman, Dr. Sumrall has raised up churches and taught the Word of God for more than sixty years. In addition he maintains headquarters for LeSea Global, and LeSea Broadcasting (international radio and television) in South Bend, Indiana, where he resides with his wife, Louise, and pastors Christian Center Cathedral of Praise. His three married sons, Frank, Stephen, and Peter, are also involved in the ministry.

Dr. Sumrall, a prolific author, has written more than 110 books and teaching syllabi. Besides his writing, he is founder and president of World Harvest Bible College, and television host on "LeSea Alive" and "The Lester Sumrall Teaching Series."

A powerful and dynamic speaker, Dr. Sumrall ministers God's message with authority and takes advantage of electronic media to reach the world today. He founded LeSea Broadcasting, Inc., which owns and operates eight television stations in the following cities:

WHMB TV-40   Indianapolis, Indiana

WHME TV-46   South Bend, Indiana

KWHB TV-47   Tulsa, Oklahoma

KWHE TV-14   Honolulu, Hawaii

WHKE TV-55   Kenosha, Wisconsin

KWHD TV-53   Denver, Colorado

KWHH TV-14   Hilo, Hawaii

K21AG TV-21   Maui, Hawaii